The Teaching Of Art

- The Vocational Program In Home Economics -

By

Florence Fallgatter

SECTION I

INTRODUCTION

> All art is life made more living, more vital than the average man lives it—hence its power. Taste, unlike genius can be acquired; and its acquisition enriches personality perhaps more than any other quality.—E. DREW.

Professor Whitford [1] bases his book, An Introduction to Art, on two hypotheses: "(1) That art is an essential factor in twentieth century civilization and that it plays an important and vital part in the everyday life of people; (2) that the public school presents the best opportunity for conveying the beneficial influence of art to the individuals, the homes, and the environment of the people."

In keeping with this present-day philosophy, the introduction of art instruction into the public schools is increasing. Through the influence of home economics, a field of education in which there is an urgent need and wide opportunity for practical application of the fundamental principles of art, art instruction is finding its way into many of the small schools as a definite part of the vocational programs. Whitford [2] refers to this present-day trend in home economics as follows:

> At first there was very little articulation between the courses in art and the courses in industrial art or household art. At the present time we realize that these courses are all related, and all work together through correlation and interrelation to supply the child with those worth while educational values which aid in meeting social, vocational, and leisure-time needs of life.

Not until all girls in the public schools can have their inherent love for beauty rightly stimulated and directed may we look forward to a nation of homes tastily furnished and artistically satisfying or of people who express real genuineness and sincerity in their living.

With the inception of the vocational program in home making through the passage of the Smith-Hughes Act by Congress in 1917, art was recognized as one of the essential related subjects. Thus, in the majority of the schools that have organized vocational homemaking programs, art has been included as a part of these programs and an effort has been made to apply the principles of art to those problems in everyday life in which beauty and utility are factors. The aim has been to develop in girls not only an understanding of these principles but also an ability to use them intelligently in solving many of their daily problems. Therefore the teaching of art in home economics courses is primarily concerned with problems of selection and arrangement. The girl as a prospective home maker needs to know not so much how to make a pattern but how to choose one well; not how to make a textile print but how to select and use it; not how to design furniture but how to select and arrange it; not how to make pottery but how to select the right vase or bowl for flowers. At the same time, teachers of related art in vocational schools have endeavored to show that true art is founded upon comfort, utility, convenience, and true expression of personalities as well as upon the most perfect application of art principles. Considerable emphasis has been given, therefore, to a consideration and utilization of those material things that afford opportunity for self-expression. The importance of such self-expression is stressed in the following words by Clark B. Kelsey: [3]

> The home expresses the personalities of its occupants and reveals far more than many realize. It stamps them as possessing taste or lacking it. Thinking men and women want backgrounds that interpret them to their friends, and they prefer that the interpretation be worthy. They also want them correct for their own personal satisfaction.

In art courses that are related to the home, an attempt is made to build up in girls ideals of finding and creating beauty in their surroundings and to bring them to the point where they can recognize fitness and purpose and see beauty and derive pleasure from inexpensive and unadorned things that are available to all homes.

Mr. Cyrus W. Knouff [4] has well expressed something of the importance of such a practical type of art training as follows:

Show the people through their children that one may dress better on fifty dollars, understanding art principles, than on five hundred dollars not understanding symmetry, design, color, harmony, and proportion. With this knowledge you furnish a lovelier home on five hundred dollars than on five thousand without it. Get your art away from the studio into life. Teach your children the gospel of beauty and good taste in their letter writing, their picture hangings, their clothes, everything they do.

Since the vocational program also provides class instruction for women who have entered upon the pursuit of home making, as well as for girls of school age, there has been some opportunity to extend art training to these women through adult classes. An attempt has been made in classes in art related to the home, home furnishing, and in clothing classes to give a training which will help them to better appreciate the influence upon family life of attractive and comfortable homes, of careful selection and arrangement of home furnishings, and of intelligent purchasing and selection of clothing.

For the girls who have dropped out of school and have entered upon employment, part-time classes have been organized under the vocational program. To these the girls may come for a definite period each week to secure such instruction as will further extend their general education, better prepare them for their present work, and also improve their home life. To the extent that the employed girl improves her personal appearance, makes her living quarters more attractive, and enjoys the finer things of life she is more valuable to her employer and is an asset to society. Much has been accomplished in this direction but there is a large opportunity in most of the States for more definite attention to such needs of the employed girl.

Section II

PURPOSE OF THE BULLETIN

> The aim of related art education is to develop appreciation and character through attempting to surround one's self with things that are honest and consistent as well as beautiful.—GOLDSTEIN.

The vocational programs in homemaking are designed for girls over 14 years of age in the full-time day schools, many of whom do not complete high school or do not have opportunity for more than a high-school education; for those young girls, 14 to 18 years of age, who having dropped out of full-time school can attend the part-time schools; and for women who are in position to attend adult homemaking classes. The provision of time in the programs for related subjects as well as for home-economics subjects covered in these three types of schools has made it possible to develop the principles of art and science as more than abstract theories. In this way these principles become fundamental to the most successful solving of many of the problems in home economics. The fact that these principles may be applied repeatedly in many different home-life situations means in turn a very much better understanding and subsequent use of them.

Through the comparatively few years in which these vocational programs have been in operation, teachers in all States have attempted with some success to give an art training that is both practical and vital to young girls and women. They have, however, been confronted with many baffling problems. Some of these have been considered by committees on related subjects and an urgent request was made by one of these committees that a more detailed discussion of these problems be published. It is the purpose of the bulletin to point out some of the most significant problems in connection with art courses that are related to the work in homemaking and to present the pooled thinking of various groups upon them to the end that girls and women may know how to make their homes attractive even with limited incomes and how to choose and wear clothing effectively and becomingly. Some of the questions to be answered in an attempt to solve these problems are:

1. What should be the place of art in the homemaking program?

2. What are pupils' greatest art needs?

3. What classroom training will help meet these needs?

4. What are the best methods to use in teaching art?

5. To what extent will laboratory problems function in meeting pupils' needs?

6. What results should be expected from art training in the homemaking program?

7. How can these results be measured?

In vocational programs the courses or units in art related to the home are taught by both art teachers and home-economics teachers. In the larger schools they are frequently assigned to the regular art teacher, provided she has had sufficient contact and experience in homemaking to give her the necessary background for making the fundamental applications. In this case she follows very closely the work in the homemaking classes and makes use of every opportunity for correlation of her art work with the home.

In the smaller schools in which the vocational programs are organized there is usually no special art teacher and therefore the home-economics teacher must give all of the art work. In most States training in art is included among the qualifications for vocational home-economics teachers. The teacher-training institutions are providing instruction in art and also special methods courses in the teaching of related art in public schools in order that their prospective teachers may be as well prepared as possible to handle the related art as well as the home-economics courses.

This bulletin is intended as a help to teachers of related art courses, be they regular art teachers or home-economics teachers, to art instructors and teacher trainers in colleges, and to supervisors of home economics. The following tabulated suggestions indicate how it may be of service to these four groups:

CHART 1.—*Suggestions for use of this bulletin by teachers*

Groups	Uses
Art and home economics teachers in vocational schools.	1. As a guide in determining objectives in related art. 2. As a help in selecting content. 3. As a means of determining method. 4. As suggestive of ways for evaluating results. 5. As suggestive in the selection and use of illustrative materials. 6. As a guide for reference material.
. Art instructors in colleges.	1. As a means of becoming familiar with some of the typical problems which prospective teachers of related art will meet. 2. As a guide in selecting those phases of art for college courses which will enable the prospective teacher of art to solve many of her teaching problems.
I. Teacher trainers.	1. As an index to the interests and needs of girls in home-economics classes. 2. As a means of determining the phases of art that most nearly meet the needs of girls. 3. As suggestive of methods for student teaching in classes in art related to the

		home.
		4. As a basis for guiding student teachers in collecting and preparing illustrative material.
		5. As a guide for reference material.
7.	Home economics supervisors, State and local.	1. As a stimulus to promote more courses or units in art.
		2. As a stimulus to work for better programs in related art.
		3. As a guide in developing art units with teachers through individual, district, and State conferences.
		4. As a basis for giving assistance to teachers on art problems.

While the major emphasis in the bulletin is directed toward the teaching of related art, mention should be made of the importance of environment as a potent factor in shaping ideals and developing appreciation of the beautiful. Constant association with things of artistic quality and frequent opportunity for directed observation of good design and color should be provided for all home-economics students. The home-economics laboratory offers an opportunity for centers in which interesting and artistic groupings may be arranged. These tend to eliminate much of the formal school atmosphere and provide a more typical home environment. Such centers in home-economics laboratories have been appropriately called appreciation centers. A laboratory with examples of the beautiful in line and color, such as well-arranged bowls of flowers, bulletin boards, wall hangings, or book corners, may prove an effective though silent teacher.

It would be futile to attempt to make most school laboratories too much like homes, however. Such attempts may give the appearance of being overdone. The light and cheerful room, with the required furnishings well arranged and one or more appreciation centers, is usually the more restful and attractive. From daily contact with this type of room girls unconsciously develop an appreciation of appropriateness and of orderliness and an ideal for reproducing interesting arrangements in their own homes. It is desirable to have the appreciation centers changed frequently, and to give pupils an opportunity to share in selecting and making the arrangements.

Figure 1.—An arrangement of wild flowers and grasses and a few books placed on a blotter on a typewriter table in front of an inexpensive india print may furnish a colorful spot in any schoolroom. Note the effective use of the screen in concealing a filing case

Section III

DETERMINING CONTENT FOR A COURSE IN ART RELATED TO THE HOME

Taste develops gradually through the making of choices with reference to some ideal.—HENRY TURNER BAILEY.

PLACE OF ART IN THE VOCATIONAL PROGRAM IN HOME ECONOMICS

In recent years, many schools carrying the vocational program in home economics have scheduled courses in related art five to seven periods each week for one semester and in some cases for an entire year. In other schools, the entire vocational half day has been devoted to home economics, art being introduced in short units or as a part of some unit in home economics where it seemed to meet particular needs.

A unit of several weeks or a full semester of consecutive time devoted to the teaching of art as related to the home is generally considered more effective than to teach only certain art facts and principles as they are needed in the regular home economics units. Since art is recognized as fundamental to the solving of so many homemaking problems, it seems desirable to provide for this training as early in the first year of the home-economics program as possible so that it may contribute to the instruction in the first unit in clothing and home furnishing.

Prior to selecting the pattern and material for a dress, the girl needs to understand certain principles of design and color which will enable her to choose wisely. If art training has not preceded this problem in the clothing course, or if there is no provision for art work to parallel the clothing instruction unit, it becomes necessary to introduce some art training at this point. A similar situation arises in connection with the other units involving selection and arrangement such as home furnishing or table service. If art is taught only to solve specific problems as they arise the pupil will not have an opportunity to apply it to other phases of home-economics instruction and will therefore fail to develop the ability to understand and use the principles of art effectively in solving her other problems. There is the further danger that the girl's interest in home economics will be destroyed by interrupting the home-making instruction to teach the art needed for each unit. For example, if the girl is planning to make a dress, her interest and efforts are centered on its production. If preliminary to starting the dress, time must be taken to establish standards for the selection of the pattern and materials, the process of making is prolonged and the girl's interest in the art lessons and in the later construction of the dress is only half-hearted.

Training which provides for many applications of the art principles as they are developed gives the girl an ability to use these principles in solving the problems which arise at other times in home-making units. It is preferable therefore to arrange the vocational program so that the art instruction parallels or precedes those units in homemaking in which there is particular need for art. However, if the program can not include the teaching of art as a consecutive unit paralleling or preceding certain units in homemaking, it will be far better for the home-economics teacher to include art training as it is needed in the homemaking work than to omit it or attempt to proceed without the basic fundamental information necessary for the successful solution of many problems in home economics. In such a plan, time and opportunity should be definitely provided later in the homemaking program to summarize and unify the art training that has been given at various times in order that it may function in the lives of the pupils to a larger extent than that of solving only the immediate problems for which it was introduced. Such a summarization will make possible the application of the essential principles of art to a wide variety of situations and will mean not only a more thorough understanding of these principles but a more permanent ability to use them in achieving beauty and satisfaction in environment.

There are then three possible plans for including art instruction in the vocational program in homemaking, namely:

1. By presenting the course in art related to the home as a separate semester or year course that parallels the homemaking course. When

it is a semester course, it is well to offer art the first half of the year in order that it may be of greatest value to the first units in clothing.

2. By giving the course in art related to the home as a separate unit in the homemaking course. Such an art unit should precede that homemaking unit in which there is greatest need as well as opportunity for many applications of the principles of art which are being developed. This will usually be the unit in clothing or home furnishing.

3. By giving short series of art lessons as needs arise in the homemaking course. Certain dangers have been pointed out in this plan. If used, it should include a definite time for unifying and summarizing the art work at the end of the course.

OBJECTIVES FOR THE TEACHING OF ART

In the vocational program in which the teaching is specifically designed to train for homemaking, it is obvious that the major objective in the related art units should be to train for the consumption of art objects rather than for their production. Bobbitt [5] elaborates on this objective as follows:

> * * * the curriculum maker will discern that the men and women of the community dwell within the midst of innumerable art forms. Our garments, articles of furniture, lamps, clocks, book covers, automobiles, the exterior and interior of our houses, even the billboards by the roadside are shaped and colored to comply in some degree, small or large, with the principles of aesthetic design. Even the most utilitarian things are shaped and painted so as to please the eye. * * *
>
> It would seem then that individuals should be sensitive to and appreciative of the better forms of art in the things of their environment. As consumers they should be prepared to choose things of good design and reject those of poor design: and thus gradually create through their choices a world in which beauty prevails and ugliness is reduced to a minimum.

This does not require skill in drawing or in other form of visual art. It calls rather for sensitiveness of appreciation and powers of judgment. * * * The major objectives must be the ability to choose and use those things which embody the higher and better art motives. Education is to aim at power to judge the relative aesthetic qualities of different forms, designs, tones, and colors. Skill in drawing and design does not find a place as one of the objectives.

The type of furnishing and decorating products consumed in the home as well as the type of clothing purchased for the family depends upon the understanding and appreciation which the home makers have developed for good art qualities. This in turn is dependent upon training. As one writer points out 6—

* * * one's capacity richly to enjoy life is dependent upon one's capacity fully to understand and participate in the things which make up life interests. In art this is particularly true, for we can only enjoy and appreciate that which we are able to understand. Through training we may be able to appreciate and understand art even though we can not produce art to any great extent. This we may think of as mental training.

The content of an art training course may be defined in terms of objectives to be attained and these in turn should be determined through a careful consideration of the art needs of girls and women. In order to know these needs, the teacher must study the appearance, conditions, and practices in the homes of her pupils. Through observation of the general appearance and clothing of the pupils and a knowledge of their interests and activities outside of school, she will obtain much valuable information, but, in addition, it is highly desirable that she visit their homes. This first-hand knowledge of the homes and community should be secured early in the school year and prior to the art unit or course if possible. The teacher should also be constantly alert to the many opportunities offered through community functions, local stores, and newspapers for becoming more familiar with particular needs and interests in her school community.

In making contacts in the homes and community, it is essential that the teacher use utmost tact. Few homes are ideal as they are, but something good can be found in all of them. The starting point should be with the good features and from there guidance should be given in making the best possible use of what is already possessed. *It would be far better for the girls to have no art work than to have the type of course that develops in them a hypercritical attitude or that creates an unhappiness or a sense of shame of their own homes. The aim of all art work is to develop appreciation, not a critical or destructive attitude.*

Through such a study of girls' needs and interests certain general objectives will be set up for units of courses in related art. Through a well-planned program the majority of pupils in any situation may reasonably be expected to develop—

1. A growing interest in the beauty to be found in nature and the material things of their environment.

2. Enjoyment of good design and color found in their surroundings.

3. A desire to own and use things which have permanent artistic qualities.

4. An ability to choose things which are good in design and color and to use them effectively.

Out of these general objectives for all related art work, more specific objectives based on pupils' immediate needs and interests are essential. In terms of pupil accomplishment these objectives may be as follows: [7]

I. Interest in—
    1. Finding beauty in everyday surroundings.
        a. In nature.
        b. In man-made materials and objects.
        c. In art masterpieces.
    2. Making homes attractive as well as comfortable.

II. Development of a desire for—
1. Beautiful though simple and inexpensive possessions.
2. Skill in making artistic combinations and arrangements in home and clothing.

III. Ability to—
1. Select and make balanced arrangements.
2. Select articles and make arrangements in which the various proportions are pleasing.
3. Select and use articles and materials which are pleasing because there is interesting repetition of line, shape, or color.
4. Select and use articles and materials in which there is desirable rhythmic movement.
5. Select and make arrangements in which there is desirable emphasis.
6. Arrange articles in a given space so they are in harmony with the space and with each other.
7. Select colors suited to definite use and combine them harmoniously.

IV. Appreciation of good design and color wherever found.

These specific objectives probably cover those phases of art for which the average homemaker has the greatest need. In the limited amount of time that is available for the related art units in most vocational programs, the choice of what to teach must be confined to the most fundamental facts and principles of art only. The problems through which these are to be developed may be drawn for the most part from actual situations within the girls' own experiences. It should be remembered that the ulterior motive in all art training in the homemaking program is to give to girls that which will make it possible for them to achieve and to enjoy more beauty in their everyday lives. In the average class few, if any, girls will have that type of "creative ability" possessed by great artists, but all of the group may be expected to attain considerable ability in selecting, grouping, and arranging the articles and materials of a normal home and for personal use. This may rightfully be termed creative ability. For example, the girl who works out a successful color scheme through wise selections and uses of color in her room or in a costume is indeed a creator of beauty.

ESSENTIAL ART CONTENT

A very careful selection of content for the course or unit in related art must be made. The vast amount of material in art from which to choose makes the problem the more difficult. An attempt to teach with any degree of success all of the content in art books and to give pupils an understanding of all of the art terms would be futile and would result in confusion. In the time available for art in the day vocational schools, as well as in the part-time and adult classes, the teacher is limited in her choice of content and must be guided by the objectives for the course that represent the girls' needs in their everyday problems of selection and arrangement.

Teachers are often baffled by the seeming multiplicity of terms. The Federated Council on Art Education has recently issued the report of its committee on terminology. The pertinent section dealing with indefinite nomenclature is here quoted: [8]

> The subject of terminology in the field of art is extremely broad and for the most part indefinitely classified. Over 100 technical terms are in common use in the vocabulary of art. Often words are used by different authors with entirely different meanings, and in other cases the degree of difference between words is too slight to warrant use of a separate term. Also many of the terms are used interchangeably by different authors and frequently they are ambiguous and obscure in meaning and difficult to apply in public-school work.
>
> In general, the literature used as a basis for planning, organizing, and developing units of art instruction in the schools is very indefinite in regard to nomenclature. For this reason the committee on terminology centered the first part of its investigation upon a

program of analysis to determine, if possible, the most significant words in common use.

In the preparation of this bulletin, several art texts, reference books, and courses of study were examined for the purpose of determining the art terms that were most frequently used. On that basis, from these various sources the following were listed:

> Balance. Proportion. Repetition. Rhythm. Emphasis.
> Harmony. Color. Line. Light and dark. Unity. Radiation.
> Opposition. Transition. Subordination. Center of Interest.
> Dominance.

Since the content for a course in related art should contribute very definitely to the girl's present and future individual and home needs it is suggested that only the minimum essential terminology be used, remembering that in such a course the chief concern is the development of those principles and facts that contribute to the realization of such objectives as have been suggested.

There seems to be common agreement that balance, proportion, repetition, rhythm, emphasis, harmony, and color are of first importance in their contribution to beauty and that the various principles and facts concerning each should be developed in an art unit or course. The selection of these seven phases of art as fundamental is supported by Goldstein, [9] by Russell and Wilson, [10] and by Trilling and Williams. [11]

The committee on art terminology has also given emphasis to these in the classification as set up in Table V of their report. This is here given in full.

Simplest form of classification [12]

Basic elements	Major principles	Minor principles	Resulting attributes	Supreme attainment
Line. Form.	Repetition.	Alteration. Sequence.		

			Harmony.	
	Rhythm.	Radiation.		
Light and Dark. } Tone.	Proportion.	Parallelism.		Beauty.
		Transition.		
	Balance.		Fitness.	
Color.		Symmetry.		
Texture.	Emphasis.	Contrast.		

It will be noted that repetition, rhythm, proportion, balance, and emphasis are listed as major principles. It will also be noted that harmony is classified as a resulting attribute. This will be the inevitable result if the principles of the first five are well taught. Arrangements which meet the standards of good proportion, which are well balanced and which are suited to the space in which they are arranged will be harmonious.

Although color is designated as a basic element of art structure in this table and the principles of design function in the effective use of it, there are some guides of procedure in the use of those qualities of color, such as hue, value, and intensity, which should be developed to insure a real ability to select colors and combine them harmoniously.

Line is also considered a basic element of art structure. Since the problems in a course in art related to the home are largely those of selection, combination, and arrangement, the consideration of line may be confined to its effect as it provides pleasing proportions, is repeated in an interesting manner, or produces desirable rhythm.

The omission of the remainder of the art terms that were found to be frequently used in art books and courses of study is not as arbitrary as it seems. Through the consideration of the qualities of color it will be found that value includes the material often given under "light and dark" or "notan."

Referring again to the report of the Committee on Art Terminology, [13] "unity" is considered as a synonymous term for "harmony." Since it is possible for an arrangement to be unified and still be lacking in harmony, the latter term is used in the bulletin as the more important and inclusive one. There is less obvious need for the principles of "radiation," "opposition," and "transition" in problems of selection and arrangement. The Goldsteins refer to them as methods of arranging the basic elements of lines, forms, and colors in contributing to the principles of balance, proportion, rhythm, emphasis, and harmony. Thus some reference to them may be made in the development of the principles of harmony and rhythm.

Emphasis has been chosen as an inclusive term which represents "subordination," "center of interest," and "dominance."

It is hoped that these suggested phases of art to be included in a course or unit in art related to the home will not be considered too limited. Each teacher of art should feel free to develop as many of the principles as are needed by her groups, remembering that it is far better to teach *a few principles well* than to attempt more than can be done satisfactorily.

In developing the principles of design certain guides for procedure or methods in achieving beauty will be formulated. For example, in considering balance, pupils will soon recognize that the feeling of rest or repose that is the result of balance is essential in any artistic or satisfying arrangement. Their problem is how to attain it in the various arrangements for which they are responsible. Thus guides for procedure or methods of attaining balance must be determined. Such guides for obtaining balance may be—

1. Arranging like objects so they are equidistant from a center produces a feeling of rest or balance.

2. Unlike objects may be balanced by placing the larger or more noticeable one nearer the center.

It will be seen that these are also measuring sticks for the judging of results. It is evident that in a short course in art a teacher can not assist girls in all situations at home in which balance may be used. Therefore it is essential that the pupils understand and use these guiding laws or rules for obtaining balance in a sufficient number of problems at school to gain independence in the application of them in other situations. Some authorities [14] term these methods for attaining results, guiding laws for procedure, or principles.

HOME SITUATIONS FOR WHICH ART IS NEEDED

The common practice in art courses relating to the home has been to draw problems from the fields of clothing and home furnishing. This has been true for the obvious reason that an endeavor has been made to interest the girl in art through her personal problems of clothing and her own room. Since in a vocational program the objective is to train for homemaking, it is essential that art contribute to the solving of all home problems in which color and good design are factors. In the selection and utilization of materials that have to do with child development, meal preparation and table service, home exterior as well as interior, and social and community relationships, application of the principles of art plays a large and important part.

One of the teacher's great problems is that of determining pupil needs. Although homes vary considerably in detail, there are many similar situations arising in all of them for which an understanding of the fundamental art principles is essential. It is important that the problems and situations utilized for developing and then applying again and again these fundamental principles shall be within the realm of each student's experience. The following series of topics may suggest some of the situations that are common to most homes and therefore be usable as the basis for problems in developing principles of art or for providing judgment and creative problems. In most of these topics, other factors such as cost, durability, and ease of handling will need to be considered in making final decisions, for art that is taught in relation to the home is not divorced from the practical aspects of it.

Child development—
    Choosing colored books and toys for children.
    Choosing wall covering for a child's room.

Choosing pictures for a child's room.

Placing and hanging pictures in a child's room.

Selecting furniture for a child's room.

Determining types of decoration and desirable amounts of it for children's clothing.

Choosing colors for children's clothing.

Making harmonious combinations of colors for children's clothing.

Choosing designs and textures suitable for children's clothing.

Avoiding elaborate and fussy clothing for children.

Meal planning and table service—

Using table appointments that are suitable backgrounds for the meal.

Choosing appropriate table appointments in—

    Linen.

    China.

    Silver.

    Glassware.

Using desirable types of flowers or plants for the dining table.

Making flower arrangements suitable in size for the dining table.

Selecting consistent substitutes for flowers on the table.

Choosing containers for flowers or plants.

Using candles on the table.

Deciding upon choice and height of candles and candlesticks in relation to the size and height of the centerpiece.

Determining when to use nut cups and place cards.

Choosing place cards and nut cups.

Arranging individual covers so that the table is balanced and harmonious.

Folding and placing napkins.

Considering color and texture of foods in planning menus.

Determining when and how to use suitable food garnishes.

Home—Exterior—

Developing and maintaining attractive surroundings for the house.

Choosing dormers, porches, and porch columns that are in scale with the house.

Grouping and placing the windows so they are harmonious with each other and with the house.

Planning suitable and effective trellises and arbors.

Recognizing limitations in the use of formal gardens and grounds.

Determining the use of the informal type of grounds.

Choosing house paint and considering how it may be influenced by neighboring houses.

Determining the influence of the color of the house on the choice of color for the porch furniture and accessories and for awnings.

Selecting and arranging porch furniture and accessories.

Selecting curtains for the windows of the house which are attractive from the exterior as well as from the interior.

Determining desirable shapes for trimmed hedges and shrubbery.

Selecting shrubbery and flowers that will contribute, at small cost, to the appearance of a home.

Planning the grounds of a home and the possible use of a bird bath, an artificial pool, or a rock garden.

Home—Interior—

Securing beauty rather than display.

Selecting textures that suggest good taste rather than merely a desire for display.

Choosing wall coverings that are attractive and suitable backgrounds for the home.

Selecting rugs for various rooms.

Selecting furniture that adds attractiveness, comfort, and convenience to the home.

Determining relation of beauty in furniture to the price of it.

Choosing window shades, curtains, and draperies from the standpoint of color, texture, design, and fashion.

Selecting appropriate accessories for the home.

Determining when to use pictures and wall hangings in the home.

Choosing pictures and wall hangings for the home.

Placing rugs, furniture, and accessories in the home.

Arranging and hanging pictures and wall hangings.

Determining the relation of type and arrangement of furnishings and accessories to the formality or informality of a room.

Avoiding formal treatment and shiny textures in the average home.

Planning how color may be used and distributed effectively in a room.

Determining how color schemes of rooms are affected by size, purpose, and location.

Discouraging the use of cloth, paper, and wax flowers and painted weeds in the home.

Social and community relations—

Determining social and community activities with which high school girls are asked to assist and for which art training is needed.

Making attractive and suitable posters for special occasions.

Selecting and arranging flowers and potted plants for various occasions.

Planning, selecting, and using appropriate decorations for special events.

Wrapping gifts and packages attractively.

Choosing and using appropriate stationery, calling cards, place cards, and greeting cards.

Clothing—

Determining appropriate clothing for all occasions.

Planning clothing that adds to rather than detracts from the charm of the wearer.

Planning to avoid garments and accessories that may be liabilities rather than assets.

Recognizing the relation of the "style of the moment" to the choice and combination of the clothing for the individual.

Choosing colors for the individual.

Utilizing bright colors in clothing.

Selecting harmonious color combinations in clothing.

Selecting and using textile designs in clothing.

Selecting and adapting style designs in patterns for the individual.

Improving undesirable body lines and proportions through the wise choice of clothing.

Selecting clothing accessories—

Hats.

Shoes.

Hosiery.

Gloves.

Bags.

Jewelry.

Selecting and using appropriate jewelry and similar accessories with various ensembles.

Choosing texture, color and design for undergarments that make appropriate and attractive foundations for the outer garments.

As yet no committee on related art has proceeded so far as to suggest specific content for art courses that are related to homemaking. Since this bulletin deals with the teaching of art as it relates to homemaking, teaching content is presented only in so far as it exemplifies methods or procedures and relates to objectives. It is hoped, however, that teachers will find real guidance for selecting content that will meet the particular needs of their classes through, the detailed consideration of objectives, the selection of principles, and the many suggestions that are offered for art applications that can be made in all phases of homemaking.

SECTION IV

SUGGESTIVE TEACHING METHODS IN ART RELATED TO THE HOME

> The test of a real product of learning is this: First, its permanency; and second, its habitual use in the ordinary activities of life.—MORRISON.

CREATING INTEREST

There is a general conception that art is naturally interesting to everyone. Accepting this as true, a specific interest must be developed from this natural interest for the most effective courses in art training. Whitford [15] says:

> Little can be accomplished in general education, and practically nothing can be done in art education, unless interest and enthusiasm are awakened in the student. The awakening of interest constitutes one of the first steps in the development of a pupil's natural talents.

Some teachers, in attempting to awaken or to hold the interest of girls in related art courses, have started with art laboratory problems which involve considerable manipulation of materials. A certain type of interest may be so aroused, for pupils are always interested in the manipulative processes involved in producing articles and even more in the possession of the completed products, but it may be only a temporary appeal rather than an interest in the larger relation of art to everyday living. While it is true that manipulative problems do contribute to the development of greater confidence and initiative and therefore have their place in an art course, yet the successful completion of most products requires greater creative and judgment abilities than pupils will have acquired early in the course. It is then a questionable use of laboratory problems to depend upon them for awakening the specific interest in art.

Initial interest of students may be stimulated through directed observation of the many things about them which are good in color and design or by discussion of problems which are very pertinent to girls' art needs or desires. [16] However, conscious effort on the part of the teacher is necessary to "open the windows of the world," if pupils are to develop real interest and experience such enjoyment from the beauty which surrounds them that an ideal of attaining beauty in dress and home is established. A definite plan is necessary for stimulating this interest which is said to be possessed by all. Without an interest that will continue to grow from day to day it is difficult to develop the necessary judgment abilities for solving everyday problems in selection and arrangement.

Professor Lancelot [17] suggests the following procedure as the initial steps in the building of permanent interests:

> 1. Early in the course endeavor through general class discussions, rather than by mere telling, to lead the students to see clearly just how the subject which they are taking up may be expected to prove useful to them in later life and how great its actual value to them will probably be.
>
> 2. At the same time attempt to establish clearly in their minds the relationships that exist between the new subject, taken as a whole, and any other branches of knowledge, or human activities, in which they are already interested.
>
> 3. Specify and describe the new worthwhile powers and abilities which are to be acquired from the course, endeavoring to create in the students the strongest possible desire or "feeling of need" for them.

If this procedure is followed, in the field of art the teacher will refrain from merely telling pupils that art will be of great value to them later in life. On the other hand, in creating interest it is suggested that class discussion of general topics within the range of pupil experience and of obvious need be used to awaken an interest in the value of art in their own lives.

The teacher must be sure that the topics are of real interest to the pupils. For example, which of these questions would probably arouse the most animated discussion: "What is art?" or "Arnold Bennett says, 'The art of dressing ranks with that of painting. To dress well is an art and an extremely complicated and difficult art.' Do you agree with Arnold Bennett? Why?"

Other discussions may be started by asking questions such as the following:

1. Have you ever heard some one say, "Mary's new dress is lovely but the color is not becoming to her"? Why do people ever choose unbecoming colors? Would you like to be able to select colors becoming to you? How can you insure success for yourself?

2. Movie corporations are spending great sums of money in an attempt to produce pictures in color. Why do they feel justified in making such expenditures to introduce the single new quality of color?

FIGURE 4.—In a Nebraska high school a screen was used in an unattractive corner as a background for an appreciation center

3. Do you like this scarf? This cushion? This picture? Why? Why not? Why is there some disagreement? To what extent can our likes guide our choices?

4. The class may be asked to choose from a number of vases, lamp shades, table covers, or candles those which they think are most beautiful. The question may then be asked, "Would you like to find out what makes some articles more beautiful than others?"

5. Where in nature are the brightest spots of color found? Have you ever seen combinations of color in nature that were not pleasing? How may we make better use of nature's examples?

6. Why do girls and women prefer to go to the store to select dresses or dress material? Hats? Coats? Can one always be sure of the most becoming thing to buy even when shopping in person? What would be helpful in making selections?

The classroom setting for the teaching of art plays a very important part in arousing interest. Attempting to awaken interest in art in a bare, unattractive room is even more futile than trying to create interest in better table service with no table appointments. In the first situation there is probably such a wide variation in the background and experience of the pupils and in their present ability to observe the beautiful things of their surroundings that it becomes increasingly important that the teacher provide an environment which is attractive and inviting. In the second situation the pupils have had experience with the essential equipment in their own homes and so can visualize to some extent the use of that equipment at the table. Bobbitt [18] says—

> One needs to have his consciousness saturated by living for years in the presence of art forms of good quality. The appreciations will grow up unconsciously and inevitably; and they will be normal and relatively unsophisticated. As a matter of fact, art to be most enjoyed and to be most serviceable, should not be too conscious.

Schoolrooms in which pupils spend a large part of their waking hours should provide for the building of appreciation in this way, and it is especially true in the homemaking room. Some home economics teachers have cleverly planned for students to share in the responsibility of creating and maintaining an attractive classroom as a means of stimulating interest in art. It would be well for all home economics teachers to follow this practice.

Figure 5.—The simplest school furnishings can be combined attractively. A low bookcase, a bowl of bittersweet, and a passe partout picture as here used are available in most schools

In many economics laboratories there are several possible improvements that would make better environment for art teaching. Suggestions for such improvements include:

1. More color in the room through the use of flowers, colorful pottery, colored candles, and pictures, featuring arrangements that could be duplicated in the home.

2. More emphasis upon structural lines—

  a. Pictures that are grouped and hung correctly.

  b. Attractive arrangement of a teacher's desk.

  c. Arrangement of the furniture so that the groupings are well balanced and the wall spaces are nicely proportioned.

  d. Good arrangement of materials on bulletin board.

 3. More attention to orderliness—

  a. When class is not working, orderliness in window-shade arrangement.

  b. Elimination of unnecessary objects and furnishings to avoid cluttered appearance.

  c. Tops of cases and cupboards or open shelves cleared.

 There are few seasons in the year when the teacher can not introduce interesting shapes and notes of color through products of nature. The fall brings the colored leaves and bright berries which last through the winter. Bulbs may be started in late winter for early spring, and certain plants can be kept successfully throughout the year. With such interesting possibilities for using natural flowers, berries, and grasses, why would a teacher resort to the use of artificial flowers or painted grasses?

 Morgan [19] pertinently discusses the artificial versus the real:

> Some say "What about painted weeds and grasses?" No; that is mockery. It doesn't seem fair to paint them with colors that were not theirs in life. One can almost fancy hearing the dead grasses crying out, "Don't smear us up and then display us like mummies in a museum." Remember, a true artist, one who truly loves beauty, despises imitation or deceit.

 There are several interesting possibilities for home table centerpieces to be used during the winter months when flowers are not available. Grapefruit seeds or parsley planted in nice-shaped, low bowls grow to make attractive-shaped foliage for the table. A sweetpotato left half covered with water in a low bowl sprouted and made the graceful arrangement of pretty foliage pictured in Figure 7, page 29.

Pupils are more apt to provide such plants in their homes if they see examples of the real centerpieces at school. It is, therefore, worth while for a teacher to direct a class in starting and caring for one or more types of them.

In one State a definite effort is made in planning home-economics departments to have the dining room open directly into corridors through which most of the pupils of the entire school pass at some time during the day. See figure 8, page 30.

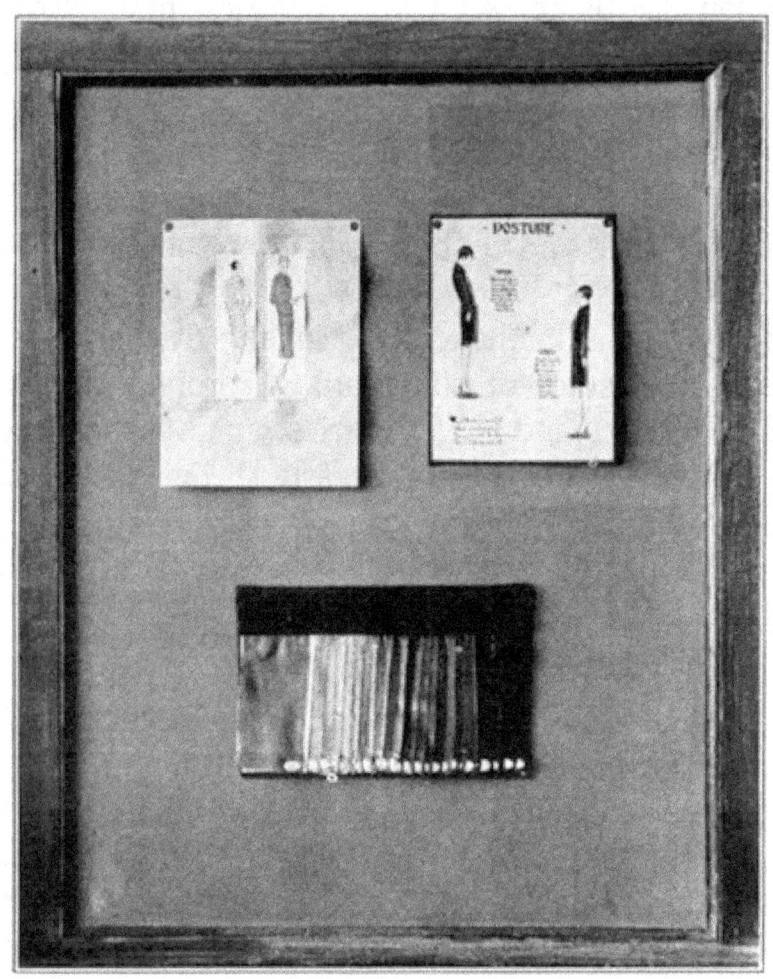

FIGURE 6.—A few pieces of unrelated illustrative materials may be grouped successfully in bulletin-board space

This arrangement permits pupils to observe attractive as well as suitable arrangements of the dining room furnishings, and especially of the table. Such a plan should be effective in establishing ideals of what is good and in raising standards in the homes of boys as well as of girls in the community.

A further contributing essential to stimulating interest in art is a teacher who exemplifies in her appearance the art she is teaching. It is said that sometimes our most successful teaching is done at a time when the teacher is least conscious of it. The teacher of an art class who appears in an ensemble of clothing which is unsuited to the occasion and in which the various parts are not in harmony with each other from the standpoint of color, of texture, or of decoration loses sight of one of her finest opportunities for influencing art practices of pupils and developing good taste in them.

FIGURE 7.—Sprouted sweetpotato produced this attractive centerpiece for the home table

There is no more applicable situation for the old adage, "Practice what you preach," than in the teaching of art. One teacher was conducting a discussion on the choice of bowls and vases for flowers as a part of flower arrangement while behind her on the desk was a bottle into which a bunch of flowers had been jammed. Contrast this with the situation in which the teacher had worked out the arrangement of wild flowers and grasses as shown in Figure 1.

DISCUSSION OF METHOD IN THE TEACHING OF ART

In discussing the best methods of teaching art, Whitford [20] says:

As a practical subject art education calls for no exceptional treatment in regard to methods of instruction. The instruction should conform to those general educational principles that have been found to hold good in the teaching of other subjects. Without such conformity the best results can not be hoped for.

FIGURE 8.—Glass-paneled doors open from the dining room directly into a main first-floor corridor in the high school at Stromsburg, Nebr.

It is anticipated that through the course in related art pupils will have gained an ability to choose more suitably those materials and articles of wearing apparel and of home furnishing which involve color and design. It is through understanding certain fundamental principles of art and using them that the everyday art problems can be more adequately solved. The teacher is confronted with the question as to how to develop most successfully this understanding and ability. Shall she proceed from the stated principles to their application in solving problems or shall she start with the problems and so direct their solution that the important principles and generalizations are derived in the process. The present trend in education is toward the second procedure and in keeping with this trend, the elaboration of method in this section is confined to the so-called problem-solving method. When pupils have an opportunity to formulate their own conclusions in solving problems and through the solution of many problems having an identical element find a generalization or principle that serves as a guide in other procedures, experience seems to indicate that they get not only a clearer conception of the principle but are able also to make greater subsequent use of it.

In their everyday experiences pupils are continually faced with the necessity for making selections, combinations, and arrangements which will be satisfying from the standpoint of color and design. Before they can select wisely they need some standards upon which to base their judgments and by which they can justify their decisions. Before they can make satisfying arrangements and combinations of material they need judgment skill in determining what to do. They also need principles or standards by which they can determine how to proceed. Finally, they need opportunity for practice so that they may become adept in assembling articles and materials into pleasing and harmonious groupings and arrangements.

The more experience pupils have in confronting and solving true-to-life problems under the guidance of the teacher, the greater is the probability that they will have acquired habits of thinking that will enable them to solve successfully the many problems that they are continually forced to meet in life.

It might be well to inquire at this point the meaning of the word problem as used in this bulletin. According to Strebel and Morehart [21]—

> Probably there is no better definition of a problem than the condition which is spoken of by Doctor Kilpatrick as a "balked activity." This idea is general enough to include all sorts and phases of problems, practical and speculative, simple and difficult, natural and artificial, final and preliminary, empirical and

scientific, and those of skill and information. It covers the conditions which exist when one does not know what to do either in whole or in part, and when one knows what to do but not how to do it, and when one knows what to do and how to do it but for lack of skill can not do it.

In teaching by the problem-solving method Professor Lancelot [22] makes use of three types of problems.

Through the first type, known as the *inductive problem,* the pupil is to determine certain causes or effects in the given situation. In determining these causes and effects, various details of information are needed but these do not remain as isolated and unrelated items. Out of the several facts is evolved a general law, a truth, or a principle. For example, in developing pupil ability to understand and use the underlying principle of emphasis, the teacher may make use of such questions as:

> Have you ever tried to watch a three-ring circus? Pupils are given an opportunity to relate their experiences.

> Have you ever seen a store window that reminded you of a circus? In which of the store windows on Center Street do you think the merchant has displayed his merchandise to the greatest advantage? Why?

From a discussion of such questions as these the teacher can lead the pupil to realize the desirability of avoiding confusion in combining and arranging articles used together and to understand at least one way of producing the desired effect.

The next type is the *judgment or reasoning problem,* which offers two or more possible solutions. In certain subjects as mathematics in which there is but one correct answer, the reasoning problem is used. In other subjects in which, in the light of existing conditions, there is a best answer, the judgment problem is used. This best answer or final choice is determined upon the basis of the law or principle established through the inductive problems. Few subjects are more concerned with the making of choices than art. For this reason, judgment problems play an important part in an art training which is to function in the daily lives of pupils. As soon as a principle has been tentatively established, it is desirable to give the pupils an opportunity to recognize the use of the principle in several similar situations and to use it as a basis for making selections. For example, following the establishment of the principle of emphasis, the teacher may ask the pupils:

> Will each of you select from these magazines an advertisement in which your attention was immediately attracted to the article for sale? Be ready to tell the class why you were attracted to this piece of merchandise.

The third and final type is the *creative problem*, which makes use of the truth or principle discovered in the inductive problems, so that the pupil is encouraged to do some creative thinking by using the principle as the basis for determining procedure to follow in a new situation. Since everyday living is full of opportunities for making choices and combinations, it is essential that both judgment and creative problems be included in practical art training. For example, to teach the use of the creative problem in the study of emphasis the instructor may say to a pupil:

> Choose a partner with whom to work. From the materials I am providing make an attractive table arrangement for a living room, and then choose a large piece of wallpaper or a textile that would make a good background for it.

Lamps, candles, candlesticks, flowers, pottery, and books will be provided for this activity, as well as the textiles and the wallpaper.

Professor Lancelot [23] sets up five standards for determining what are good problems. They must, he says, be—

1. Based on true-to-life situations.

2. Interesting or connected with things of interest.

3. Clearly and definitely stated.

4. Neither too difficult nor too easy.

5. Call for thinking of superior ability.

In addition, there are four other factors to be considered in the planning of a successful problem series;

1. Each problem should score high according to the above standards.

2. The usual sequence is in the order already given—inductive, judgment, and creative. Since the creative problems call for the highest type of thinking and are the most difficult, the natural place for them is at the end of the problem series. At that point the pupils should have sufficient information and judgment ability to enable them to solve the most difficult problem quite readily. Introducing the difficult problem too soon may discourage the pupil and lessen interest in the course as a whole. Some creative problems involve fewer art principles than others. For example, the spacing of a name on a place card is much simpler than the hanging of a picture in a given space. In art it is desirable to use simple creative problems as they fit naturally into the problem series. (See pp. 38-39.)

3. As the problem series develops, there should be an increase in the difficulty of the problems. It is obvious that the simpler problems are to be used at the first of the series. To develop judgment to a desirable extent, the later choices will be determined from an increasing number of similar situations and from situations in which the degree of difference decreases as the problem series progresses.

4. Each problem series should involve as many types of life situations as possible. For example, applications of art are needed in the various phases of homemaking. (See Section III, pp. 18-21.) For that reason it is very desirable to select problems in each series from as many of these phases as possible. By this means the pupils are better able to cope with their own problems in which a fundamental art truth, or principle is the basis for adequate solution.

The following detailed procedure is presented as an illustration of the way in which an art principle may be developed through a problem series. It may appear to be unnecessarily detailed and to require more time than the average teacher would have for planning. However, part of material here given consists of probable pupil replies and a description of the illustrative materials that are to be used.

SUGGESTED PROCEDURE FOR DEVELOPING AN ABILITY TO USE A PRINCIPLE OF PROPORTION FOR ATTAINING BEAUTY

An effort is here made to present the details of a teaching plan by which a principle of proportion may be developed by the pupils. This plan is spoken of as a lesson, but not in the sense that it is to be accomplished in a limited amount of time, such as one class period. The term *lesson* is used to designate the *entire procedure* from the introductory problem to the point where the pupils have developed the ability to use the principle of proportion. It will be possible to make more rapid progress with some classes than with others and in some class periods than in others. It is suggested that the teacher endeavor to evaluate the class time and plan so that the end of the period comes not as an interruption but as a challenge to further interest, observation, and efforts.

The lesson suggested below should take not more than three of the short class periods of 40 to 45 minutes. If too much time is spent on one series there may be a lessening of interest because of seeming repetition. On the other hand, if sufficient applications and problems are not used after the principle is established, there is danger that the pupils will not be able to use it in solving other daily problems.

Further suggestions for problems, illustrative materials, and assignments may be found on page 40.

SUGGESTED PLAN FOR THE DEVELOPMENT OF AN UNDERSTANDING OF THE PRINCIPLE OF PROPORTION AND ITS USE

General objective.—To develop ability to—
    Select articles which are pleasing because of good proportions.
    Adapt and make pleasing proportions as needed.

Specific objective.—To develop ability to—

> Divide a space so the resulting parts are pleasing in their relationship to each other and to the whole.

Assume that the group to be taught is a ninth-grade class in art related to the home. Very few members of the class have had any previous art training and such training has consisted of some drawing and water-color work in the lower grades. Previous to this lesson, it is assumed that the teacher has developed the pupils' interest in the beauty to be seen and enjoyed in the everyday surroundings of their community, and has developed pupil ability to understand and to use a principle of proportion, namely, that *a shape is most pleasing when one side is about one and one-half times as long as the other*.

The establishment of the above principle has probably given the class an opportunity to read of the Golden Oblong or the Greek Law of proportion in an art reference such as Goldstein's Art in Everyday Life. This will have served to further establish a feeling for interesting shape relationships and also will have made the pupils familiar with the term "proportion." The class may or may not have developed an ability to recognize and use the principles of balance.

Details of Lesson Procedure

> Problems and questions to introduce the principle needed to solve this and many similar problems

The first-aid room in the school is very bare and cheerless. Miss M., the school nurse, and Mr. B., the superintendent, have decided that some thin ruffled curtains at the two windows will soften the light and make the room more homelike. Miss M. has purchased some ready-made curtains and has asked if the class would like to determine the best way to arrange the tie backs. "How many of you think that this is an art problem? Will it be helpful to us to know how to divide a window space with curtains? Tie-back, ruffled curtains have been very much in vogue for some time. The models in the drapery departments and the illustrated advertisements show a variety of methods to use. Since there is so much variation, how can we be sure that curtains are tied back in the most attractive way possible?"

Use of illustrative materials

The curtains have been hung at the two windows in the first-aid room. At one window the curtains are not tied back and come to the bottom of the casing, at the other one they are arranged in two other ways designated as A and B. By the A method the curtain is tied back exactly in half; by the B method it is tied back between one-half and two-thirds of the length. The initial question would probably be: "Which of these two arrangements, A and B, do you think contributes most to the appearance of the window?"

Class discussion

Some of the class will undoubtedly choose A. Their reasons for this choice may be as follows:

1. The uncurtained window space is more or less diamond shaped.

2. The four sections of the curtains are almost exactly alike.

Others will choose B, and give such reasons as follows:

1. The window space is less noticeable.

2. There is more variety in the curtains.

3. It is more interesting if the eye can travel down the longer part of the curtain and then come to rest at the part tied back.

These reasons will probably lead the majority of the class to decide that B is more desirable than A.

At this time another arrangement designated as C may be introduced. For this, one curtain at the second window may now be tied back so near the sill that the two parts do not seem to be related. One designated as D may also be introduced, in which the arrangement is exactly like that of B, except that the curtains are tied back above the center instead of below.

Summary of class discussion

A summary of the points which may be brought out by the class on each arrangement of curtains follows:

A, in which the curtains are divided exactly in half, is not interesting for a very long time because—

1. The divisions on each side as well as above and below the tie backs are all alike.

2. It leaves too much of the window exposed.

3. The window space exposed does not follow the lines of the window.

4. The arrangement becomes tiresome the longer one looks at it.

5. One's curiosity is quickly satisfied when it is obvious that the two areas are exactly alike.

B, in which the curtains are tied back between one-half and two-thirds of the length and below the center continues to be interesting because—

1. The two sides are alike, but the top half is not exactly like the bottom half. This variation makes it more pleasing.

2. Although the top half of each side is larger than the bottom half, it does not look top-heavy because the tying back of the curtain gives a place for the eye to rest. It holds the same amount of attention as the long length of curtain above it.

C, in which the tie backs are placed at a point below three-quarters the length of the curtain, is not interesting for any length of time because—

1. The eye travels very far down the length of the window, then is suddenly interrupted by the tie back.

2. This arrangement is top-heavy.

3. The window space is not pleasing.

D is exactly the reverse of B, so it is equally interesting.

Further use of illustrative material

"Suppose we now look at these curtained windows from the outside. Do you think that the arrangements which we decided are most pleasing from the inside are equally pleasing from the outside?"

After examining the arrangements of curtains at the windows the pupils may be led to decide that B and D continue to be the most pleasing. "Since we are now agreed that in B and D the tie-backs divide the curtains so that the spaces are most pleasing, would you like to determine just where the division comes in each of the curtains?" Some of the members of the class will be eager to take the measurements and report on them. They will find that in—

Class determines best division of space

A the division is exactly in the center of the length.

B the division comes at a point between one-half and two-thirds of the length.

C the division comes at a point more than three-quarters of the length.

D the division comes at a point between one-half and two-thirds of the length.

At this point it will be well to direct the attention of the class to the possibility of space division in other places. "Do you think that there are spaces, other than windows, which could be satisfactorily divided according to the same measurements?" Members of the class may suggest panels in doors, divisions in dress, and the like.

"Marie is making a plain one-piece dress. The narrow belt is to be of the same material. Where would be the best place for her to place the belt?" Try placing a belt on a plain one-piece dress or provide three tracings of such a dress with the belt placed as follows:

In one the belt divides the dress in two equal parts.

In the second the belt is placed so the skirt is a little longer than the waist.

In the third the belt is placed at normal waistline. (With a long skirt this makes the skirt very much longer than the waist.)

Measurements may again be taken and compared with the divisions of the window. The class may be led to decide that a plain dress is divided best by a belt which comes some place a little above or below the center of the total length.

Class develops statement of principle for good proportion

"If you wanted to help someone to divide a space so the resulting parts would be pleasing, what directions would you now give them?" Each member of the class may be asked to write out a statement of directions. Some of these may be put on the blackboard and the class members given an opportunity to choose the one which they think would be most helpful in obtaining space division. The final statement should bring out the following: *When a space is to be divided the result is most pleasing if the dividing line falls at a point between one-half and two-thirds of the length divided.*

To insure real ability to use the principle of space division which has just been developed, it will be necessary to give the class several problems which they may judge as a group. These in turn should be followed by other problems which will call for individual planning and the application of the principle in their solution. The number of such problems will vary with the class, but there should be enough to insure the desired ability. Furthermore, those given should be from as varied fields as possible so that the pupils will be able to make their own applications as needed.

Series of Suggested Problems to Test Pupils' Ability to Recognize and Use the Principle of Proportion Just Developed

Judgment problems given for class solution

1. "In which of these doors do you think the division into panels is most satisfactory? Why?"

In this problem, as in the succeeding ones, the solution is not considered adequate unless each pupil can justify the choice she makes or the answer she gives according to the principle which was established in the earlier part of this lesson.

2. "On which of these book covers do you think the space is best divided? Why?"

3. "Small boxes have a variety of uses in our homes. These are all approximately the same in size. Which do you think has the most interesting relation between the depth of the lid and the depth of the box? Why?"

4. "Helen is planning to make a dress with a cape collar. Her mother thinks the collar is not deep enough and suggests that Helen change the pattern. How could she determine the most becoming depth for her cape collar?"

5. "Jane did not have enough cloth to make a dress without piecing it or buying more material. She decided to put a yoke in the waist. How deep on the waist do you think a yoke should come to be most attractive?"

6. "Mary has some 6-inch glass candlesticks at home. How can she determine the length of candle that would be most suitable when they are used on the buffet?"

Creative problem involving activity

7. "Arrange the window shades so that the window space and the depth of the shade are pleasing in their relation to each other. Justify the arrangement you have made."

Judgment problem involving activity

8. "Choose a girl with whom to work during the next few minutes. Check to see if the dresses you are wearing to-day have the belts so placed that each dress is divided as well as possible. Suggest any desirable changes for each other and justify each change."

(At some time in the development and subsequent use of the principle established in this lesson it will be well to connect it with a previously established and closely related principle. Such a connection is made use of in the following problems.)

Creative problem involving use of a principle previously developed

9. "I have an odd picture frame that I wish to use for this landscape which came from a magazine illustration. The picture is the right width, but it is too long for the frame. How do you suggest cutting it so that it can be used in this frame and still retain its pleasing proportions?"

(Such a landscape will obviously have a division of space in it by the line of the horizon. The problem will be one of retaining pleasing space divisions in the picture, as well as retaining pleasing proportions of the whole, while fitting it to the frame.)

Possible assignment

10. "Choose a plain card most pleasing in proportion, which may be used as a place card for the home economics luncheon that the class is giving to the mothers. Plan the placing of the names on these cards. Justify your choice of card and the place you have chosen for the name."

Problem 10 may well be given as an assignment. It may be given at any desired time in the problem series as a judgment problem following the establishment of the principle. A definite attempt has been made to arrange problems 1 to 8 in order of degree of difficulty. It is evident that those which necessitate creative planning and manipulation call for greater ability than the problems of selection.

Although problems 9 and 10 are given last they may be introduced at any point. They are given last here because they require the use of two principles of proportion, i. e., relation of length to width in objects and division of a space into two parts. Problems 1 to 8 make use of only one, i. e., the principle concerned with the division of a space into two parts.

Further Suggestions for Problems, Illustrative Materials, and Assignments

There are various possibilities of introducing this lesson on proportion other than through the arranging of curtains. The curtain problem is used here because it involves a school situation. Such a problem sometimes has as great an appeal for girls as some of the most personal ones. However, any one of a number of problems, such as the placing of a belt on a dress, the depth of a flounce or yoke on a dress, the relative lengths of jacket and skirt in a suit, or the length of candles for candlesticks may be used for the introductory one. Choice will be determined upon class needs and school possibilities. The important factor will be to see that the problem is so stated that it stimulates a desire on the part of the pupil for adequate solution.

If the school windows and real curtains are not available for this problem, some window and curtain models may be borrowed from drapery departments of local stores for class use. If it is not practicable to use curtains or to borrow store models, the teacher might prepare in advance of the class meeting miniature windows for this problem. These may be made of heavy construction paper, cardboard, or beaver board, and should be of a size and scale that will permit accuracy in the conclusions drawn from their use. *The use of miniatures should be confined to emergency situations, when the real things are not obtainable.*

With some classes it may be necessary to use additional illustrative materials in which there are no other factors than those of space division. The teacher may prepare rectangles of neutral paper, representing any given space to be divided, in which the division is made by a contrasting line in each of the following ways:

One divided exactly in half.

One with the dividing line between one-half and two-thirds of the length from one end.

One with the dividing line at a point three-quarters of the length.

One with the dividing line between three-quarters of the entire length and the end.

Conclusions drawn from a comparison of the above illustrative materials may in turn be applied to other problems in which color, texture, or design may have made it difficult in the beginning for the pupils to focus their attention upon space division.

It is obvious that if choosing candles for certain definite candlesticks is the introductory problem, candles of varying heights, but of the same color, will need to be provided if the class is to come to some definite conclusions. If this problem is used in the judgment series, as in the lesson above, it will serve as another application of the principles of space division.

One possible assignment has been given in the lesson. Other possibilities present themselves as follows:

1. "Where could you find an illustration in which you think there is particularly pleasing space division? Will you bring such an illustration to class?" Such an assignment affords additional training in selection and directs the observation of the pupils to their environment outside the school.

2. "When you are at home to-night, will you notice the arrangement of articles on your dresser? If these articles are not as well arranged as you think they can be, make an arrangement which is balanced and which divides the space as well as possible. Be ready to tell the class why you think you have a well-balanced and nicely spaced arrangement." In this particular assignment it is assumed that pupils have previously developed the ability to make balanced arrangements. This is a further application of that ability but in an advanced form. In developing an ability to make balanced arrangements, attention was centered on the placing of articles on either side of a center. Now that the ability to divide a space has been developed, it is time to take up

the balancing of articles within a given space so that the proportions of that space are pleasing.

It is highly desirable in the teaching of art that the relationships of principles in the attainment of beauty be established as soon as each is clearly understood. It is not enough that a principle be clearly established and several applications of it made. As soon as this much has been accomplished it is time that problems be used which involve this new principle and at least one of the preceding ones. Such a cumulative teaching plan is essential to make art training function most successfully in the lives of the pupils.

CLASS PROJECTS

Many judgment and creative problems arise in certain group and class projects, providing opportunity for utilizing and showing the relationships of the essential principles of art in their application. They are more often undertaken in connection with home furnishing than with other phases of homemaking. Provision for such projects involving the selection of articles and materials and the arrangement of them to bring about an attractive and harmonious effect can usually be found right in the school. For example, as a class project, the wall finishes, the furnishings, and the accessories may be chosen and arranged for a specific room such as the dining room, bedroom, or living room of the home-economics department if such rooms are available or the rest room for teachers or girls.

In some schools, the separate cottage is used to house the home-economics department. This offers an opportunity for pupils to show what they would do under practical conditions. It is important that the furnishings for such cottages be in keeping with what is possible in the majority of homes in the community. If when the cottage is new the teacher plans with the pupils for only the essential furnishings at first, further problems of selection and arrangement will be reserved for several classes.

In a few schools the home-economics department has cooperated with the trade and industrial department in planning small houses, which were then built by the boys in their carpentry classes. The girls have then selected and arranged the furnishings for such houses as a class project.

When there is no opportunity within the school for such class or group projects, there are other available possibilities to which a teacher of related art should be alert. Better Homes Week is observed in many towns and cities and those in charge are usually glad to turn over the furnishing of one or more rooms for the occasion to the local home-economics department. A center to which so many visitors come affords an excellent opportunity for exemplifying to the community good taste in furnishings at a cost consistent with the income of the average family.

In one school the related art class took over the project of refinishing one of the rooms in the girls' dormitory. It was necessary to use the furniture already provided, which meant the expenditure of a minimum amount of money. There was, therefore, the problem of refinishing some of the furniture to bring it into harmony with the newly planned room. The old dresser was one of the pieces to be remodeled and painted. Figures 9 and 10 show the dresser before and after the class had worked on it.

FIGURE 9.—The dresser as found in the dormitory room
FIGURE 10.—The same dresser after the class in related art
had remodeled and painted it

In a few instances, homemakers have entrusted the furnishing of rooms in their homes to the related art class. Thus it is seen that a variety of opportunities do exist. They should be located and such use made of them as will mean the enrichment and vitalization of the work in related art.

NOTEBOOKS

In the limited time usually allotted for the teaching of art related to the home the teacher is confronted with the problem of how to make the best utilization of that time. One of the first questions which must be decided is whether a portion of it shall be devoted to the making of notebooks. In analyzing the situation she will need to determine the purposes which they serve. The notebooks may be justified on the ground that they—

1. Provide a collection of illustrative and written materials which pupils may have for future use.

2. Provide a classroom activity through which pupils learn.

3. Measure pupil ability to recognize art applications through the selection of pertinent illustrations.

4. May supplement or be used in place of a class text.

5. Provide material for the school exhibit.

6. Insure material for competitive purposes at county and State fairs.

7. Maintain interest.

Answering the following questions may serve to determine whether notebooks are of value to the pupil:

1. Does the notebook provide for worthwhile individual experience?

2. Will it pay in terms of time and energy expended?

3. What is the ultimate use of it?

The following chart may serve to aid the teacher in judging whether notebooks are justified:

CHART 2.—*Analysis of the value of notebooks in art courses*

Purposes of notebook	Value		
	In terms of worthwhile individual experience	In terms of time and energy consumed	In terms of ultimate use of notebook
1. To provide a collection of material for later pupil use.	To the extent that the activities involved exercise individual judgment.	Usually more time and energy consumed than later use justifies. This is dependent upon the degree of elaborateness	Notebooks may be exhibited, but beyond that experience seems to indicate that few girls or women use

		of the notebook. Copying, tracing, and pasting are very time-consuming.	them later in home life as a source of information.
2. To provide classroom activity through which pupil learns.	To the extent that the activities involved provide opportunity for exercising selection.	Both may be well spent, provided the evaluation in (1) is kept in mind and if much of the mechanical work is done outside of class.	It may train pupils to be observant and critical and thus aid in making wiser choices in real life.
3. To measure pupil's ability to recognize art applications in the selection of pertinent illustrations.	To the extent to which the activities give added opportunity for making independent choices and offer opportunity for students to recognize and select additional applications to those given in class.	A justifiable use of time and energy, provided the emphasis is on making selection and the mechanical processes are minimized.	After selections have been made they are of no use later as a measuring device.
4. To supplement	There is little opportunity for	It is not justifiable use	Pupil may use it for

or use in place of a class text.	individual experience in writing a notebook, since the material is usually dictated or copied from references. With the present available facilities for reproduction of printed information there is little excuse for this procedure.	of pupil's time to compile text material which should be made available to them through other channels.	review in organizing subject matter of the course for examination. Beyond this, probably little use is ever made of it.
5. To provide materials for school exhibits.	Not a justifiable objective. It develops a sense of false value. Some judgment is undoubtedly developed, but the competitive spirit so far exceeds the desire to learn that the experience is frequently unfortunate to the individual.	Time and energy consumed do not justify preparing notebooks for this purpose alone. Time so used may mean sacrificing opportunities for the development and use of judgment in real-life situations.	No use except for some proud relative to show to friends the notebook that has won special recognition.
6. To insure	See (5) above.	See (5) above.	See (5)

material for competitive purposes at county and State fairs.			above.
7. To maintain interest.	To the extent that the pupils are permitted to use some originality or initiative in choosing material and compiling it, interest may be maintained.	An expensive use of time and energy, since interest may be obtained in so many quicker and easier ways. If there is seemingly greater interest it is probably in the manipulative processes rather than in art itself.	Of little value since notebooks are usually stored away and forgotten.

In the light of the analysis of their value it would seem that the use of notebooks should be carefully considered before they are given any place in the teaching of art related to the home. If used at all, they should not be the objective of the course but the voluntary effort of the pupils in attaining other objectives and should take a minimum of class time. From the standpoint of time alone there is certainly a question as to how much routine work in cutting, pasting, or writing should be permitted.

The teacher not only has a responsibility for teaching but for the most efficient teaching at a minimum cost in time and energy to the pupil. The immediate and ultimate uses of collected materials should be the most important criteria as to kind and amount. When the pupils have an opportunity to choose illustrations which show good application of art they are not only developing their powers of discrimination but are revealing the degree to which these powers have been developed. Some practices in judgment are valuable and probably sufficient in themselves. For instance, when a pupil selects two or three good examples of rhythmic movement in design she will have developed a finer feeling for rhythm and will have demonstrated her recognition of it. Of what value would it be for her to make a permanent record of these illustrations?

There are other selections that may be of more permanent value, such as pictures chosen to illustrate some art application. When these are mounted or framed attractively they make desirable additions to the girl's room and home.

Illustrations suggestive of new and interesting ways of applying trimming, or of arrangements for dressing table covers, window draperies, and similar materials are also of more permanent value. They may serve the immediate purpose of illustration in the art class and then be made available for later use if they are filed in some way. One of the most satisfactory means of keeping such materials is in large envelopes or portfolios. These may be provided at small expenditure of time and money by using heavy wrapping or construction paper. The latter may be made very simply by cutting and folding the paper to form a double-pocket envelope.

Rather than encourage the notebook type of collection of magazine illustrations and samples of materials, the teacher may interest the girls and women in selecting simple articles that may be used in their own homes and will give lasting enjoyment.

If a notebook or portfolio is to be used for keeping certain records for later reference, the requirements for it should be limited to those which are easily attainable by all members of the class. However, this does not suggest a restriction of the efforts of the especially-talented pupil. Each page of the simplest notebook offers opportunity for the application of art principles in the planning of good margins, as well as in making attractive groupings of illustrations on mounted and written pages. It would seem desirable to discourage the elaborately decorated type of notebook covers because they consume considerable time for making and have such a temporary use. Portfolios well constructed and of lasting quality may be used later for keeping choice, unmounted pictures, or photographs.

THE PLACE OF LABORATORY PROBLEMS

The "laboratory problem" is a term quite generally used to designate a problem which is carried on within the classroom and involves some pupil activity.

Such problems may involve judgment, a combination of judgment and manipulative skills, or a combination of judgment and creative thinking with some manipulation. They may be used to discover a law or principle, to verify a conclusion, or to test the judgment and creative ability of the pupils.

The term as it is used here is restricted to the type of problem which involves judgment in selection, creative planning, and careful manipulation of materials for successful completion. Such problems are frequently known as craft problems.

Since this type of problem involves so many kinds of ability it is evident that it can not be introduced too early in the course if it is to be executed successfully by the pupils. To the degree that judgment ability in selection has been developed and there has been opportunity to do creative thinking, the pupils will be able to carry out such problems more independently.

This does not mean that all laboratory problems are to be reserved until the end of the course, but it suggests that each problem be considered carefully to determine if the pupils' preceding training has been adequate. For example, posters may be undertaken much earlier than a problem in tie dyeing. The main requirement for successful posters is an ability to use the principles of proportion and emphasis. A problem in tie dyeing to be successful should be preceded by an understanding of the use of the principles of proportion, balance, and harmony as well as of color.

The successful laboratory or craft problem provides a measure of the pupil's judgment and creative ability; an opportunity for manipulative expression; and a means of producing something that should contribute to the beauty of the home. The pupil should visualize each finished article in its place in relation to the whole scheme of the room or home. The making of articles for which there is no definite need or place in the girl's home can hardly be justified in school time. The use of those materials in laboratory problems with which the pupils will need to work later is considered the more valuable experience. For example, experience in working with dyes rather than with water colors or paints will be more useful to the average girl, for in her home she is more often confronted with the problem of renewing color in underwear or other garments or changing the color of curtains to fit in with the new color scheme of her room than with problems necessitating the use of water color or paints.

Laboratory problems that are well selected and wisely directed will result in one or more of three values:

1. Pupils may have a better appreciation of fitness and purpose.

2. Pupils may have a greater desire to own and use beautiful things.

3. Pupils may have a greater appreciation for possibilities of beauty in the simple things.

With these possible values in mind the teacher will need to determine which of the many laboratory problems can be used most effectively.

The following standards are offered as a basis for evaluating the various possibilities for such laboratory problems:

1. *Time.*—This is probably the most important factor because, in the first place, many laboratory problems are far too time consuming, and, in the second place, the total time allotment for an art course is usually limited in the vocational program in homemaking. *Every article which can be justified for a school problem should require a relatively small amount of time and few repetitive practices.*

2. *Ultimate use of the article.*—This is a factor which is often lost sight of and as a result girls make ruffled organdy or embroidered or quilted silk pillows for which they have no real use. *Every article should be evaluated in terms of its relation to use and surroundings and be chosen for a specific place.*

3. *Structural quality of the article.*—"Structural design is the design made by the size and shape of the object." [24] Laboratory problems involving structural design afford opportunity to make use of several art principles, but to bring about structural beauty the pupil must have achieved real ability to use these principles. *Every article should meet the fundamental requirements of good design.*

4. *Suitable decoration for the article.*—"Decorative design is the surface enrichment of a structural design." Too often decoration has failed to contribute to the appearance or to the utility of the article. *Decoration, if any is used, should make a lasting contribution rather than a temporary appeal.*

5. *Good technique.*—An article may be well planned, with good design and pleasing decoration, and may be one that would not require too much time in the making, but the finished product may not be acceptable because of poor technique. *Laboratory problems should require only that type of technique which can be achieved successfully by the pupil.*

The ultimate purpose of this particular part of the training in art related to the home is to enable girls and women to make selections for their homes that will contribute to their attractiveness rather than to produce artisans in the various crafts. Therefore the selection of class laboratory problems must be made most carefully. The teacher will need to emphasize repeatedly the importance of structural value, as well as the utility of articles if the pupils are to appreciate these qualities as more fundamental than decoration.

Difficult situations often arise as a result of poor choices on the part of pupils for their laboratory problems or for the decoration of articles to be made. Great tact is required in leading pupils to see that such choices are poor without offending them. It sometimes means slow progress and waiting until the class judgment brings out opinions that may have more weight than those of the teacher. It is more effective for a teacher to allow a pupil to proceed through the "trial and error" method than to completely discourage the making of the poorly-chosen article. However, the successful teacher must evaluate each situation in light of the cost in time and money and the effect that failure would have upon the individual pupil. The most important consideration is that out of the experience the pupil will progress toward the desired objectives.

The "trial and error" procedure is well illustrated in the following report of a Wisconsin high school teacher:

> Related art is taught in all units but is taken up in detail for the first time in the sophomore year in home furnishing and decoration, wardrobe planning, and the Christmas gift unit. Most of the girls come from very poor homes; and the prevailing idea of beauty is largely artificial flowers or large framed family photographs.
>
> The aim in the related art work has been to help the girls use the things they already have and to appreciate beauty in the things they own and have the opportunity to buy or see.
>
> The following problem arose in the sophomore class of 27 girls in the home furnishing and wardrobe planning unit:
>
> The girls were to make Christmas gifts in which their knowledge of design and construction was to be applied. The gifts were to be for some particular member of the family or friends. After deciding what they were to make they planned the design and colors. Some of the girls used yarn or bias tape designs on theatrical gauze or monk's cloth, making scarfs, pillows, curtains, davenport covers, or couch covers. Others made collar and cuff sets, aprons, underwear, towels, laundry bags, pan holders, or passe partout pictures.
>
> Elva came to school with a blue bird panholder to embroider in many colors as her gift to a married sister. I told her it would take much time and I wondered if it were worth while putting the time on a panholder. I asked her if the design were appropriate, and she said she liked it better than the plain quilted holders.
>
> I did not know what to do as I did not want her to spend time on such a foolish and inappropriate article but decided that she might be convinced of her poor choice after making it so I allowed her to work on the holder, giving her help as needed, but no encouragement as to the beauty of the holder. In order that the

others in the class might be more convinced concerning some of the things we had discussed in our related art from this holder, I asked each girl to keep accurate account of time spent in making the gifts.

The girls who were making plain holders had finished a set of them and at least one other simple gift while Elva continued embroidering on her holder. Everyone was much interested in all of the gifts and made many comments. Although none but Elva knew my views, she received no class approval or bursts of enthusiasm over her holder, and one girl even ventured to ask her if she thought her holder was good design.

Finally the gifts were finished, and each girl exhibited her work, criticizing it both constructively and adversely. Finally it was Elva's turn. It was a pleasant surprise when she said: "I spent 6-1/2 hours of time on this one holder, and I don't like it now. I could have made six plain ones, and they would have been better in design and served the purpose better than this one will. I don't think my sister will appreciate this holder more or maybe as much as one of the others."

The class did not take exception to her criticism, and we then evaluated the design, appropriateness, and time spent on it. The class decided Elva was right in her conclusions that she had made a mistake.

As most of the girls were giving their gifts to persons in the community, we discussed placing and use of the various gifts, and the girls decided that after Christmas they would tell how or where the gifts were being used. When this time came and Elva reported, she said the panholder had surely been used and was so badly scorched that you couldn't even see the design that took 6-1/2 hours.

Several laboratory problems which teachers have used in art classes are here presented. In the light of the standards which are offered as a basis for determining what problems shall be chosen, they are discussed briefly as to their educational possibilities. The order in which they are listed is alphabetical and not suggestive of importance in ranking.

1. *Block printing.*—If the designs are so simple that the girl learns how to adapt similar simple designs to other things for her home, this problem may have value in such a course. In addition, the girl is acquiring a wall hanging or a table cover that will have an appropriate place in her home. Such simple blocks may be kept for using on a variety of articles for gifts which the girl can make at very little expense and in a short time. The "stick printing" also offers some opportunity for adapting designs.

2. *Fabric or yarn flowers for the wardrobe.*—If such articles are made of appropriate materials, there is opportunity for girls to exercise judgment in the selection of colors, textures, and combinations that are suited for their use on special garments.

3. *Hand stitchery (embroidery, hemstitching, fagoting, and quilting).*—In so far as the pupils can justify the use of hand stitchery for a particular article or garment and then confine their efforts to the choosing and adapting of designs, to the planning of color combinations and to the doing of just enough of the stitchery to learn the process, stitchery problems may have a place in the art course. The actual repetition of stitches is too time consuming for class practice. Unless the pupils will finish such problems outside of class some others would better be chosen. There is an opportunity through stitchery problems to show girls how a bit of appropriate handwork may be applied to an inexpensive ready-made garment, thereby enhancing its attractiveness and value.

4. *Lamp shades.*—Lamp shades may be individual class problems if the pupils have real need for them. If made in class the educational value comes through planning the size and shape, choosing suitable and inexpensive materials, and adapting appropriate designs to them.

5. *Lettering.*—Since in many real situations in life one is requested to print one's name, it would seem desirable to include some very simple straight-line printing problems.

6. *Marbleized paper.*—This is a possible class exercise which involves the handling of colors. Such papers may be utilized as wrapping for gifts, book covers, desk sets, or portfolios.

7. *Painting furniture.*—There will probably be little opportunity or need for the actual carrying out of such a laboratory problem in the beginning course in art related to the home, but it may be used successfully in a later unit in home furnishing or in a home project. The educational value in painting furniture is confined to the choice of finish and color and in learning the manipulative processes. The actual painting of many pieces is too time consuming to be done at school and too laborious for young girls to do unassisted at home.

8. *Place cards.*—The choice of size and shape of card and the placing of the name on it are the important factors in using plain place cards. Here is an opportunity for girls to make use of straight-line letters. In selecting and making decorated place cards, suitability to purpose and kind and amount of decoration are other factors that need to be considered.

9. *Portfolios.*—Simple portfolios may be appropriately used as class problems provided the pupils have a need for them. They afford opportunity for the application of the principles of proportion, emphasis, and harmony as well as of color. If decoration is to be used, it should be simple and suited to the material of which the portfolio is made and to its intended use.

10. *Posters.*—When the need for posters arises, a related art class may profit by applying their knowledge of color, emphasis, and space arrangement in making them. For a simple yet attractive poster, a well-mounted picture which suggests the story with one or two lines of lettering may be grouped to form a unit. This takes but a short time. For those students having difficulty in making the straight-line letters in crayon or ink, the gummed or cut letters may be used, or a school stamp lettering press may be utilized.

11. *Rug hooking.*—The educational value of this problem is in the selection and adaptation of designs and colors to the spaces and materials used. Beyond this point it is largely repetitive manipulation;

and unless girls want to finish rugs outside of class, and will have an opportunity to do so, such work should be discouraged.

12. *Tie dyeing.*—If good dyes are procurable and the exercise is limited to using a few hues, tie dyeing may be desirable from the standpoint of developing ability to combine colors successfully and to the fitting of the design to the shape of the piece dyed. If used as a class problem, special attention needs to be given to the adaptation of design to the space. This means careful preparation of the material for the dye bath. Wise planning for the desired color effects is also essential.

Shaded dyeing offers an interesting opportunity for further use of color. The problem involves the recognition of interesting ranges of values and the determination of pleasing space relations for those values.

It has been suggested previously that handling dyes would be a more valuable experience to girls than using paints or water colors. However, to insure success, dyes of standard quality should be selected and carefully prepared. Soft water has been found best for most dyes. A soft, loosely woven material without dressing is typical of the fabrics that are most frequently dyed at home and may well be used at school. Carefully dyed yard or half-yard lengths of cheese cloth have been found valuable in supplementing other fabrics in the study of color. The experience girls gain in mixing and handling the dyes for these short length pieces has been deemed by some teachers as far more valuable than that gained through making flat washes for a color chart as a means of understanding colors and their relationships.

Much time is usually lost in having pupils attempt to mix paints for flat washes for the various hues of color charts. The purpose of making color charts is to provide the girls with a guide for recognizing and combining colors. Many teachers have found that a more successful method is to have the pupils arrange colored fabrics or papers in the order of their hue relationship. It has not been considered necessary for each pupil to do this, since the ability to recognize hues and their relationships may be equally well achieved through working in groups. A large chart of standard hues provided by the teacher will be valuable in developing understanding of color.

13. *Weaving.*—This problem requires a loom, and for the small amount of weaving that should be done in school and in view of future needs, the teacher is seldom justified in asking for such a piece of equipment.

Book ends, trays, and candlesticks are essential articles from the standpoint of utility and well-selected ones are valuable as illustrative material in the development of good judgment in their selection and arrangement. When these articles are used as laboratory problems, special care should be taken to avoid placing the emphasis upon decoration.

There are no doubt other problems that may be used successfully. However, only those should be chosen that will supplement the art training advantageously and that will measure up to the five suggested standards on pages 47-48, which, stated in more specific terms, are—

1. Every article should require a relatively small amount of time and few repetitive practices.

2. Every article should be evaluated in terms of its relation to use and surroundings and chosen for a specific place.

3. Every article should meet the fundamental requirements of good design.

4. Decoration, if any is used, should make a lasting contribution rather than a temporary appeal.

5. All problems should require only that technique which can be achieved successfully by the pupils.

FIELD TRIPS

Field trips in some form have been used to quite an extent in the teaching of many subjects and have been undertaken for a variety of reasons. In the teaching of art the purpose may be fourfold:

1. To stimulate interest in beauty.

2. To provide contact with materials and articles as they are to be found in life.

3. To extend information.

4. To provide additional opportunity for exercising judgment.

Unless the trips to be made by the class are planned carefully they may become merely freedom from regular school routine. If the group has an opportunity to help plan the trip, including the route to be taken, the points of interest to be looked for and reported upon at the next regular meeting of the class, the conduct to be maintained on the trip, and the courtesy due the homemaker or the merchant or the business man who is cooperating with the class visit, there is bound to be greater interest and concentration upon the trip with more beneficial results.

Trips taken very early in the unit or course can do little more than serve as a means of stimulating interest in the new phase of work. Trips taken later may be used to verify conclusions and develop judgment in making selections as well as to create broader interests.

One class in a study of clothing selection made several trips to the local stores. The first one was preceded by a study of surface pattern in dress fabrics from the standpoint of the effect of design and color upon the appearance of the wearer. The trip to the local stores was made to determine which of the wash dresses exhibited in three store windows best met the standards which the class had set up for such a dress. The standards were as follows:

1. The style or design of the dress should be suited to the kind of fabric and the surface pattern of it.

2. The trimming should be in harmony with the construction lines and the color of the dress.

3. The surface pattern of the material should be one of which the wearer and her friends would not soon tire.

In this particular case, since the class was small and the trip included only window shopping, some discussion was carried on in the group as they stood outside of the display windows.

At a little later time the same class was taken to the stores on a shopping trip. Each pupil was asked to select material for two dresses for one of her classmates, one to be for a washable school dress and the other for a "dress-up" dress. The materials were to be selected from the standpoint of color and design for the individual and of suitability for the type of dress. The procedure set up by the class previous to the trip was to work quietly and independently at the store and to refrain from saying why they did or did not like various things they saw there. When each girl had made her selections she was to ask the clerk for small samples and to be sure that the rest of the class saw the large pieces from which she had made her selections. During the next class period each girl exhibited her samples and justified the choices she had made. The girl for whom the selections had been made was given an opportunity to express her opinion, and the remainder of the group were encouraged to comment upon the proposed materials.

When these pupils later had the problem of selecting materials for the new spring dresses they had decided to make in class, there were many evidences that the experience gained on the trips to the stores had been of real value to them.

In the study of accessories for the spring dress this class had another window-shopping trip which followed a lesson on the selection of shoes. The purpose of this trip was to see what effect trimming lines had upon the apparent width and length of the shoes and to choose from those displayed in the windows the style of shoe that would be most suitable for some member of their class to wear with a dress she had made or purchased.

Field trips that have a definite purpose and are well planned and arranged for in advance can make valuable contributions to the classroom training in art. If a class is to be taken on a trip to a store, to visit a home in the community, or to an industrial plant it is only courteous and an evidence of good management for the teacher to obtain permission and make necessary arrangements with the merchant, the homemaker, or the manager far enough in advance to avoid conflict in time and to plan in accordance with their most convenient time for visitors.

MEASURING RESULTS

How can the degree to which art training is functioning in the lives of the girls and women be determined? It is fully as important for the teacher to evaluate results of her teaching as to plan for it carefully. This has been commonly recognized as a definite part of teaching, but the procedure has been largely limited to the giving of written tests. Such tests have usually been of the type that measure factual information and have probably failed to indicate the degree to which the student's life has been improved by her use of the art information.

Tests which are thought provoking and the solving of school problems are both valuable measures, but they are not sufficient in themselves for testing art. They fail to reveal whether or not the girl is making voluntary and satisfactory art applications or appreciating beauty to any greater extent in her everyday life. Whitford [25] refers to outcomes as follows:

> Two significant and fundamental outcomes of art education are revealed by an analysis of the relation of this subject to the social and occupational life of the pupil. These are, first, ability to recognize and appreciate art quality and to apply this ability to the needs of everyday life; and, secondly, ability to produce art quality even though in a relatively elementary form.

When art has been effectively taught there are many tangible evidences of its functioning in the personal and home life of the girl. What are some of these tangible evidences that indicate successful art training? The outstanding ones may be found in the girl's appearance at school and in the choice and arrangement of furnishings in her room and home.

Evidences of the Successful Functioning of Art in the Classroom

Improved personal appearance of pupils may manifest itself in their selection of ensembles from garments already possessed or from newly selected garments from the standpoint of—

1. Color combinations.

2. Texture combinations.

3. Appropriateness of clothing for school.

4. Appropriateness of style of garments to the girl.

5. Appropriateness of accessories.

The story of freckled-faced Mary well illustrates how art did function in one girl's life. She was an unmistakably plain high-school girl. Her hair was red, her face freckled, and her nose decidedly retroussé. Her clothes of gaudy colors never fitted and always seemed to emphasize her personal deficiencies. But one day a new teacher came to the school, whose business it was to teach home economics, and into her hands Mary, mercifully, came. A few months later the State supervisor of home economics, a close observer, visited the school, and her attention was soon drawn to Mary, not as the worst-looking girl in the school but as one of the best-looking girls in the school. Soft, becoming colors, good lines, and a suitable style of garments had brought out the best tints in her red hair, softened the freckles, and transformed a plain girl into an attractive one. All of this had been accomplished as an indirect objective of the teacher in her related art instruction in home economics. Mary had unconsciously learned that beauty is, after all, a relative term in regard to individual objects and that it is the setting that gives grace and charm.

Unless the teacher is on the alert some interesting evidences of successful teaching may go unnoticed. Some of the changes in the pupil's appearance come about gradually and without audible comment. Such was the case in one class. Most of the year Betty had been wearing an old 1-piece wool dress. During the winter she had worn a belt of the dress material at a low waistline, so that the belt covered the line at which the pleats were stitched to the dress. Early in the spring, and, as it happened, near the beginning of the art unit, Betty evidently became much interested in the styles that advocated a return of the normal waistlines and succumbed to the appeal of the new leather belts in the store window. For several days she proudly wore a wide leather belt fairly tight and high, with this straight flannel dress, all unconscious of the fullness bunching above the belt, the poor proportions of the dress, and the poorly finished seam where the pleats were joined to the dress. After some time had been spent on the art unit in which no direct reference had been made to Betty's belt, the teacher was very much pleased one morning to notice that Betty had taken in the side seams of her dress to remove some of the fullness and was wearing the leather belt a little more loosely and somewhat lower, so that the space divisions of the dress were more pleasing. Is there a better evidence of successful art training than that which shows that the pupil is able to adapt in an attractive way the garments of her present wardrobe so that they measure up to the individual's desire to be up to date?

A Kansas teacher reports that she overhears comments among girls before and after school which reveal evidences that art is influencing tastes. Here are some examples of these comments:

> That color is too bright for her.

> That particular green dress makes her skin look yellow.

> Those beads harmonize beautifully with that dress.

> She is one girl who should not wear her belt high. It makes her look so short and dumpy.

> I have given my sister my colored scarf, which I now realize clashed with everything I had, but fits in with her things.

Better pupil contributions to class work constitute another evidence of the effectiveness of art instruction. These manifest themselves in—

1. Voluntary reports and comments of observations and experiences.

2. The bringing in of illustrative material for class and bulletin board use.

3. The asking of relevant questions.

Some of these may be evidenced outside the regular class period. This was true in the case of Joan, a high-school freshman in an art class, who had been rather unwilling at times to accept the art standards set up by the rest of the class. Her argument was, "What difference does it make? Why can't everyone select just the things she likes?" Very little attention was definitely directed to her for she would sulk if pressed for a reason to justify her statement that everyone should choose as she liked.

One Monday morning the teacher, upon her arrival at school, found Joan waiting in the classroom to tell her of the shopping trip she had had with her mother on Saturday. Joan had selected a red silk dress which she and her mother had both liked. After going home Joan had begun to wonder if the dress would look all right with her last year's coat and hat and wanted to know what kind of hose would be best to wear with the dress. This teacher could well feel that her art teaching was developing in Joan a real interest in art.

Assumption of greater responsibility by the pupils for more attractive arrangements at school contribute another evidence of the effectiveness of art instruction. This may manifest itself in the arrangement of—

1. Articles on tables, buffets, or bookcases.

2. Flowers in suitable bowls.

3. Books and magazines.

4. Exhibit cabinets.

5. Stage settings for class plays.

Still another criterium of the effectiveness of art instruction is the spread of interest in the work from home economics pupils to others in the school.

A teacher of related art in Missouri says:

> One of the most striking and pleasing evidences of art's carrying over is the fact that so many girls outside of the home-economics department come in and ask questions regarding some of our pupils' clothing or ask to see the art work done here. The seniors in the teacher-training department are especially interested, as they expect to teach art in the rural schools and have had practically no work in it.

Evidences of the Successful Functioning of Art in the Home

One of the most gratifying results of art teaching is the influence it creates in improving the homes of the community. This may be seen through—

1. More attractive arrangements and rearrangements of furniture, rugs, pictures, and accessories.

2. Elimination of unnecessary bric-a-brac.

3. More suitable use of color.

4. More appropriate choice of textiles and texture combinations.

5. Improved selection and care of shrubbery, hedges, and flower beds. Removal of unnatural or grotesque shapes.

6. Improvements in walks, trellises, fences, and gates to make them more suitable for house and grounds.

A teacher in a vocational school in North Dakota reports as follows:

> One of the most valuable evidences of improved practices that I see from our art work is the girls' appreciation of things that are beautiful and their desire to acquire a few truly beautiful things for their own rooms and homes.

An itinerant teacher trainer describes a lesson in related art which she observed. It is given here for its very practical suggestion of a means for measuring results of teaching:

> The day before my visit the teacher had taken all the girls of her class to a city about 18 miles away to purchase Christmas gifts for their mothers. The girls had limited themselves as to possible types of gifts within their limited means and at the same time suitable for their mothers. Only one gift cost more than $1 and that was the joint gift of two sisters to their mother. The class had agreed that each gift should be of such nature that the application of art principles studied would be involved in making a choice. They had practically confined themselves to pictures, beads, book ends, or vases.

> All of the gifts had been brought to the home-economics rooms for storage until the Christmas tea when they would be presented to the mothers.

The girls brought out all their purchases and all entered into the judging without false modesty. In some cases the purchasers were able to suggest improvements in future purchases.

The entire group showed unusual poise, self-confidence, and good judgment, as well as tact, in making suggestions.

The new problem arising from this lesson of designing an invitation to the annual Christmas tea for the mothers was a very real one to the girls. The principles of balance were taught and applied, and the girls decided on a design for the invitation.

Various tests and problems may also serve to measure the results of art teaching. A description of the test which was used at the end of one art unit, as a basis for determining the use the pupils were able to make of that training, is here included. It is hoped that this plan may prove suggestive to other teachers.

The test was given at the close of an art unit which had been conducted according to the method described earlier in this section. (See Section IV, pp. 34 to 42.) The class consisted of ninth-grade girls and met for daily class periods, 80 minutes in length.

At the beginning of the period on this day the teacher told the class that the first part of the period was to be devoted to a make-believe shopping trip. In this test, cost was not a factor but the material used did not include too wide a range in values. Slips with the names of the articles for which they were to shop and directions were prepared. Some of the shopping was to be done individually and some of it by groups. When all were finished the shoppers were to meet in the classroom and be given an opportunity to see all of the "purchases" and to know why each selection had been made. The slips were then passed out from which the pupils were to draw. The directions for procedure on the slips were as follows:

1. Select from the box of scarfs the one you think would be most suitable to wear with the blue coat that is in the clothing room. (Three girls drew copies of this slip and worked together in choosing the scarf and justifying the final choice.)

2. For the plain tailored flannel school dress hanging in the clothing room, select a scarf or some appropriate accessory which could be worn with the dress to introduce variety. (Three girls worked on this shopping problem.)

3. Mrs. B. wishes to use this colored picture and these blue-green pottery candlesticks in an arrangement on her mantel. She does not know what color of candles to buy. She is afraid that if she uses blue-green candles the color combination will be monotonous. Which of these candles would you suggest? Why? (There was considerable variation in the candles provided. In addition to several hues from which to select there were plain as well as decorated candles, and some variations in length. Two girls made this selection.)

4. Suppose your bedroom were a small one and had but one window in it. Select from these samples the wallpaper design that you think would make the room look larger and the material to use for draperies in the room. (A large wallpaper sample book and several samples of plain and figured fabrics in a variety of colors were provided for the two girls who did this shopping.)

5. You are to have a new print dress. Which of these pieces of material would you choose as having the most rhythmic design? Which trimming material do you think would be best to use with it? (Several samples of printed materials were pinned together and each pupil who drew a copy of this slip was given a separate set from which to choose. Bias tape, braid, and lace, as well as plain and printed fabrics, were provided for trimmings.)

6. Choose from these printed fabrics the one that you think would be most suited in color and design for some member of this class. Tell for whom you have made the selection, justify your choice, and suggest the trimming that you think would be most appropriate. (The selections were made from a miscellaneous group of samples, printed and plain materials in a variety of colors.)

7. From colored fabrics plan three color combinations that could be used for a dress. Describe the combinations that you have used in each as to hue, value, and intensity, indicating areas of each color and justify

their use together. (An assortment of fabrics separate from those used by other pupils was prepared for this group to save time and to enable the pupils to work independently. If fabrics are not available, papers may be used, although colors are never the same as in fabrics.)

As soon as the "purchases" were all completed the pupils individually or as group representatives, exhibited the selections to the class and gave the reasons justifying each choice. The entire class participated in commending or criticizing the selections made and the reasons given. Here the teacher was able not only to measure the individual's ability to solve a given problem but to observe how readily the pupils could recognize desirable selections and offer correct art reasons as the basis for those selections.

Immediately following the reports, the pupils took their places around the tables in the clothing laboratory, and the remainder of the period was devoted to individual and written judgments of materials which were passed around the class. This material was numbered, and to each piece was attached a slip of paper containing suggestive questions and directions as follows:

1. To which of these mounted pictures do you think the margins are best suited? Why? (The pictures cut from magazines were suitable for the classroom or a girl's room and were mounted on a neutral construction paper. Only one had margins suited to the size and shape of the picture.)

2. Which of these stamped and addressed envelopes do you think has the most pleasing margins? Why? (Several envelopes differing in size and shape were addressed and stamped in a variety of ways.)

3. Which of these dress designs are balanced? Select one that you have decided is not balanced and suggest the changes necessary to make it so. (Illustrations of several dress designs that the pupils themselves might use were chosen from a current fashion sheet and were mounted and numbered. Attention was first focused on the designs which were balanced and then on the possibility of improving those that were not balanced.)

4. In which of these pieces of china do you think the design is in harmony with the shape of the dish and would make a suitable background for food? Justify your choice. (In the absence of real china, magazine advertisements of china furnished the necessary examples from the standpoint of color and design.)

5. Which of these three border designs has rhythm made most beautiful? Why? (Advertisements of towels with borders furnished the designs.)

6. Is this calendar pleasing in proportion? Give reasons for your answer. (The calendar was quite a long rectangle in shape, but the margins were well suited to it, and the entire space was well divided.)

7. What in this picture catches your attention first? How has the artist emphasized it? (The picture used was one taken from a magazine cover and was a copy of a painting of recognized merit.)

8. Which of these fabrics has the most pleasing combination of stripes? Why is that piece more pleasing than the other two? (Cotton materials were provided with stripes varying from those that were regularly repeated at intervals as wide as the stripes, to those in which there was an interesting grouping of stripes of varying widths.)

9. Which of the containers pictured in this advertisement would you select to use for an arrangement of flowers? Why? (The containers varied from those which were undecorated and well proportioned, to those which were elaborate in shape as well as in surface decoration.)

10. On this page are two color combinations. Tell what scheme has been used and by what means the colors have been harmonized. (These combinations were cut from magazine advertisements in which the combinations were pleasing. The colors had been harmonized through the quality of each color as well as the area.)

In each of the above situations the answer was not considered adequate if the pupil had merely made a choice. A reason was needed to substantiate that choice and the most complete answer was based on the principles of art which applied in each case. This did not mean that formal statements of the principles were required. It was considered much more desirable to have the pupils give in their own words the art reasons which justified each choice.

That such a test gives pertinent evidence of the use pupils are able to make of their art training is shown in the words of the teacher who gave the above test:

> I did not want my students to feel that art work was something to be memorized until the course was over but a thing to be carried through life. I was very much pleased with the results I obtained from the class. The pupils responded to the idea that art could be used in every phase of life even when it came to writing up their daily lessons. They no longer thought of art as something accomplished only by professional artists, nor the word as meaning painting and drawing, but as the feeling or appreciation of things beautiful in line, design, and color. By having them constantly put into practice the art principles which they learned, by the end of the art unit the pupils had enough confidence in themselves to back up each choice that they made with a reason. I felt that this type of a test was a true test of their art knowledge because it was practical.

Immediately the question arises as to the source of materials to use in such a test, for it is evident that those used as illustrative material for developing or applying principles in class can not be reused in the test.

For questions 1, 2, and 3 of the first part (p. 59) the materials used may be borrowed from a store or solicited from interested friends. The girls themselves may be asked in advance to bring in a scarf and some dress accessory. Since the choice is confined to an article suited for a particular garment that choice ceases to be a personal one, although some pupil-owned garments and accessories are used. Drug stores, paint shops, and drapery departments may be solicited for wall paper catalogues and samples of fabrics. Some firms will send fair-sized samples or swatches of material for class use.

In the second part of the test (pp. 60-62) magazine illustrations and advertisements proved to be most usable. Illustrative materials have long been recognized as having an important part to play in the teaching of home economics. The possibilities of their use in testing the results of teaching have not yet been fully appreciated. Further suggestions on illustrative materials will be found in Section VI, page 75. The objective type test also has its place in measuring results. 26

As has been suggested, many tangible evidences of the effectiveness of art instruction may be observed and several of them can be noted in the classroom. Others of equal or greater importance can not be measured in the classroom, but can only be determined by the teacher as she visits the home, supervises home projects, and participates with her pupils in the life of the community. The home project has been an essential part of the vocational program in home economics since the inauguration of the vocational program in 1917-1918. It has afforded an opportunity for extending the work of the classroom into the home and has developed additional desirable abilities through practice under normal conditions. The project carried on in the home has therefore been considered a valuable educational procedure.

It is also a measure of results of teaching in that it shows how well the girl is able to apply classroom training to actual situations that arise in her project. Art can contribute to the success of many home improvement and clothing projects. There has been a tendency in some cases, however, for the pupil's interest in the actual manipulative processes involved in the project to be so great that she lost sight of the opportunities for the best applications of art.

In the home project "Redecorating my room," there is evidence that the pupil has consciously applied art for the successful attainment of it. This project, reported as follows, grew out of the unit in home furnishing, which is recommended as an additional study following the first general course in art related to the home.

Name of project.—Redecorating my bedroom.

Plan of project.—Since my bedroom must be repapered and painted, I plan to make it as attractive as possible by following some of the things we have had in our art work in home economics.

The plaster of the walls is not suitable for painting, so I will select some light and cheerful colored paper with figures in warm pastel shades.

The woodwork, which is a pea-green color, is quite dull and cool for a north room and needs brightening up, so instead of having the same color again, I will paint it a light cream or ivory. A dark-yellow paint covers the floor, which is quite worn in some places. I do not like this color, so my plan is to use either light brown or tan, at least something darker than the walls, as I want the floors darkest, the walls next, and the ceiling the lightest.

To make the furniture, which is now varnished, blend with the color of the woodwork and floor, it too will have to be painted a color lighter than the floor or darker than the woodwork.

In place of white tie-back curtains, deep cream or some other color darker than the white will be more suitable with plain-colored draperies, as they will blend with the ivory woodwork and enameled furniture.

In order to contrast the curtains with the bedspread and dresser scarf, I think the spread and scarf can be a lighter cream color.

A cushion for the rocker and a flower by the window will also add color and finishing touches to the room.

Outline of project activities.—

Jobs	References
Selected wall paper and	Looked through several

helped paper the room, using paper with light background and pastel figures in it.	wall paper catalogues and samples at the furniture store.
Painted the woodwork an ivory color.	I got sample folders of paint and also used the samples in the catalogue.
	The House and Its Care, by Matthews.
Painted the floor an inside tan (deep tan color).	Used sample folders of paint.
	Goldstein, Art in Everyday Life, for suggestion on color.
Painted the furniture with beige enamel.	I referred to paint folders.
Made an unbleached krinkled spread, repeating the color of the draperies on the spread.	I looked through several magazines and catalogues for styles and my mother and sister gave suggestions.
Made deep cream voile curtains. These were straight curtains, not ruffled.	Studied different styles of curtains in magazines.
Made draperies.	Referred to magazines and catalogues.
Made cretonne cushion for rocker.	Mother gave me suggestions.
Made a dresser scarf, repeating colors that are in the wall paper.	Consulted mother and my teacher.

Time for project.—A total of 62-1/2 hours was spent on my project between November 15 and January 11.

Story of my project.—My bedroom is a northeast room, long and narrow, with sloping walls, and had but one window on the north side. This made it dark and cheerless during most of the year. Last summer my father built a dormer window in the east side of the sloping walls. Immediately the room seemed transformed. It did not look so long and narrow and the sunshine drove out the darkness and cheerlessness. This improvement gave me the idea of remodeling the bedroom, and I saw many possibilities of making it into a cheerful and cozy one, where I could spend much of my spare time.

I began almost immediately to remodel. The first thing I started with was the walls. They were not suited for painting, so I chose paper, which I got at the furniture store. After looking through several wall paper catalogues I chose paper with a light background and an inconspicuous, conventionalized design in pastel tones of blue-green, red-orange, violet, and yellow. (Sample attached.)

Before I put the paper on the wall I cleaned and sandpapered the woodwork, floors, and dusted the walls. Father and I then began papering. We had some trouble in matching the paper, but after the first two strips were matched the rest was put on without difficulty. The next job was painting the woodwork. I applied two coats of ivory paint after having dusted the wood so that there would be no dust to interfere with the painting. This was done successfully and without difficulty. (Sample of color used.)

The next step was painting the floor. I chose inside tan. (Sample of color used.)

The furniture was easier to paint than the floor but it took quite a while to give it two coats. I used enamel that dried in two hours, so had to be careful not to rebrush the parts I had painted, as rebrushing causes light streaks after the paint has set. (Sample of color used.)

With father's assistance, I completed the difficult work of papering and painting. Then I began the pleasant work of making a spread, curtains, draperies, and cushion.

I looked through several magazines, catalogues, and books for the different ways of making curtains, spreads, and draperies. My mother and sister also gave suggestions as to what would go best with the room and how to make them. I chose deep cream voile curtains with red-orange (peach) pongee draperies. The curtains are made with a wide hem at the bottom and sides.

The spread is of unbleached krinkled muslin. (Sample attached.) I have a deep ruffle of the same material at both sides and I repeated the red-orange color in two bands near the ruffle.

The rocker needed a cushion. This I made of figured cretonne, which blends nicely with the room. (Sample attached.)

On the floor I have two rag rugs which also have colors of blue, red-orange, and tan.

My teacher came to visit my room one evening and gave me some splendid ideas.

I shall add a homemade wardrobe for my clothes and put a low shelf in it for my shoes. In front of the dormer window a table will fit nicely. I am going to fix this table up with some books supported by book ends, a simple box, and a blooming plant. I will keep some simple and useful articles on my dresser.

All through this report there are many evidences that the pupil can apply the principles of art successfully and also that she knows how to obtain further information as needed. Another interesting feature of this project is that the pupil did not consider this a finished piece of work when her original plan had been completed. She saw other possibilities for her room and was beginning to make plans for further changes and additions in keeping with those that had been completed. There is no better evidence of the success of art training than in the effective use the girl makes of it in her home life. It may be anticipated that a girl who has gone this far in improving a part of the home will endeavor to make other desirable changes. To the extent that the members of the entire family welcome the changes brought about by the project and enjoy the results, the project may be considered successful.

The success of art instruction may then be evaluated by—

1. Evidences in the classroom.

2. Evidences in the home.

3. Tests which call for judgment and creative thinking.

4. Home projects.

HOME PROJECTS

Home projects involving the use of art are to be encouraged, not only as a device for measuring the results of teaching, but as a means of stimulating applications of art in the home. Art training will function in the immediate lives of the girls to the extent that successful applications of it are made through the home projects. However, such applications are not made without the ideal and therein lies the importance of developing in girls ideals of having and creating beauty that will be sufficiently deep seated not only to motivate but to carry through pieces of work in their homes that will bring more beauty and satisfaction to the families. Projects carried on in the home demand more than a repetition of certain processes that have been learned in school. They involve the bringing together of many principles and processes, the exercising of judgment in determining which are needed, and then the applications of these in the new situation. Thus the home project is a creative piece of work.

Much more use of art should be encouraged in many of the projects which girls are choosing in all phases of home activities since it can contribute so much to the comfort and attractiveness of homes, and these are essential factors of happy family life. Lewis Mumford,[27] a distinguished critic of modern architecture and decoration, has fittingly said:

> The chief forms of decoration in the modern house will be living things—flowers, pictures, people. Here is a style of interior

decoration that perpetually renews itself. For the modern house is built not for show but for living; and the beauty it seeks to create is inseparable from the personalities that it harbors.

It is safe to predict, on the basis of the home projects in which desirable art applications have been made, that through conscious effort the following outcomes may be expected:

1. The ideal of creating beauty in the home will be strengthened.

2. Pupils will recognize greater possibilities for making art applications.

3. Pupils will become more observing and discriminating.

4. Family life will be bettered by those projects in which home improvement has been achieved.

5. Pupils will appreciate that beauty is not dependent upon cost.

6. More successful projects will be carried out.

The last point is reflected in the summary of results that one girl made of her home project, "Improving the Looks of My Room." She said:

> The only cost for my project was for the two little pictures that I hung by the mirror. I learned that it is not always the cost or quality that determines the attractiveness of a room. Things must be arranged correctly or much of the beauty is lost.
>
> My mother thought that everything I did to my room was an improvement and encouraged me to do much more. I am planning to do more for our entire house in the future.

The home project which resulted in an improved kitchen in one home had a favorable influence upon the home life of the family. The girl, with the financial assistance of her brothers, had made an attractive and more efficient kitchen in the bare 4-room house, which was the home of the family. The living quarters were naturally limited in such a small space. In reporting on this project the teacher said:

I feel that this project has been very worthwhile to Ethel and her whole family. Her mother was so grateful and told me how much better it made her feel to walk into a bright, cheerful kitchen every morning. She said that her boys were so pleased they had made a living room out of the kitchen on cold winter nights.

Suggestive Home Projects in Which Art is an Important Factor

Clothing projects which include planning as well as construction offer many possibilities. This planning would necessitate such applications of art as the adapting of style, design, and color to the individual, selecting and combining textures and colors in the fabrics, and using appropriate trimmings and accessories. Such projects would also afford opportunity for exercising judgment through the evaluation of results. The same opportunities exist in the "make-over" projects as in the others in which all new materials are used. A few clothing projects involving art are suggested, as follows:

1. Planning and buying or making (*a*) school wardrobe for self; (*b*) season's wardrobe for small sister or brother.

2. Making the most of clothing on hand. This will involve cleaning, pressing, and mending, as well as some remodeling.

3. Remodeling clothing on hand and choosing additional garments needed for an attractive and suitable wardrobe.

4. Selecting the accessories to complete a costume for self or for mother.

Home-improvement projects which involve the exterior of the home as well as the interior should have a place in the home-economics program. In this group of projects there is not only great opportunity for the application of art as the basis for planning and selecting, but also for the making of more pleasing arrangements of things already in the home. In view of the fact that in most home-improvement projects the girl needs to make the best use of furnishings and equipment already possessed by the family, and usually has a limited amount of money to spend, her problems are greatly increased. Except in the few cases in which she has the privilege of newly furnishing a room or a part of the home, the starting point is with the present possessions in the home and a careful evaluation of them to determine the good in each. *She should appreciate the fact that the home and its possessions belong to the entire family and that any changes she may desire to make should meet their approval or at least be undertaken with their consent.* In most cases the proposed changes will be more welcomed by the family if little outlay of money is necessitated and if the largest and best use is made of cherished household treasures.

Joint home improvement projects have been carried out in some States with considerable success. In these projects the girls in home economics have worked cooperatively with brothers who were in agricultural classes. This usually meant greater interest on the part of parents and other members of the family. More ambitious programs for improvement were thus possible, not only through greater family support and encouragement but through the boy's ability to make certain alterations in structure or finishing that a girl could not do alone. Through these projects the boy and girl have learned much from each other. Perhaps the most conspicuous evidence of success has been the spread of interest beyond the homes into community improvement.

Some suggestive home-improvement projects are as follows:

1. Making the home kitchen a more convenient and attractive place in which to work.

2. Arranging home furnishings and accessories so that harmony, balance, and desirable centers of emphasis contribute to the attractiveness and comfort of each room.

3. Assisting in the selection and arrangement of furniture, wall coverings, floor coverings, or accessories for the girl's own room or other rooms in the house.

4. Preparing the sun porch for summer use.

5. Planning and caring for window boxes.

6. Planning and planting a flower garden or border that will contribute to the appearance of the home and also be a source of pleasure.

7. Re-covering or making slip covers for furniture.

8. Assisting in the selection of linen, china, silver, and glassware for the table.

9. Planning the table decorations for special occasions.

10. Keeping appropriate centerpieces of flowers, plants, or fruit on the home table.

Two home-improvement project reports on Beautifying Our Yard and Improving Our Home are given as suggestive of types of projects in which art plays an important part in successful achievement. Only the plans for the first one are given, since they show the significant art applications.

Name of project: Beautifying Our Yard

(Reported by a girl in a vocational high school in Nebraska.)

I. Reasons for choosing this project—

1. The flowers will improve the looks of the yard.
2. It will be an experience in the arrangement of flowers for me and will not only add to the attractiveness of the yard but to the house and surrounding buildings.

II. Aims—

1. To make the yard and house more attractive.
2. To keep flowers watered and weeded and give other care they need.
3. To plant the flowers in the most suitable place and position.

III. Plans—

1. Get all the information I can from experienced gardeners and from books and magazines that tell which are the best flowers to raise,

easiest to grow and take care of, and when and where they should be planted.

2. Names of flowers to be planted—

    Cock's Comb. Zinnias. Phlox. Larkspur. Nasturtiums. Petunia. Sweet William. Cannas. Snap Dragons. Sweet Peas. Poppies. Heliotrope. Asters. Sweet Alyssum. Cosmos. Marigolds.

3. Location of flowers—

    a. Along the walk (both sides).

    b. Along sides of the house.

    c. Along side of vacant lot.

    d. Around garage.

    e. Along the driveway.

4. How to plant the flowers—

    a. The tallest ones in the back.

    b. The shortest in front.

5. When to plant them—

    a. Sweet peas, March 1 to 10, or before.

    b. Others in the middle of April to May.

    c. The flowers may be started in the house and transplanted to the outside when the weather permits.

6. Care of flowers—

    a. Water the flowers at least once a day (if dry weather). It is best to water them in the evening.

    b. Weed them at least twice a week and loosen the soil around them.

    c. If some insect starts destroying any of the flowers, spray them with a solution which will kill the destroyer.

IV. Approval of guardian—

This project, Beautifying Our Yard, selected by Alta, is a very profitable project, especially at this time of the year when our thoughts are directed toward the planting of flowers, shrubs, etc. A beautiful yard adds so much to the home and makes everyone more happy and contented. This project should create a desire in Alta to take more interest in the yard and in planting it. Also watching the plants grow will make her feel some responsibility in caring for them, while at the same time every member of the family will enjoy the realization of the project. I wish her all success in making this project come true.

NOTE.—An excellent planting plan worked out on squared paper accompanied this project.

Name of Project: Improving Our Home

(Reported by an Alabama high school girl.)

In the spring I took as my project home beautification. I thought when I started there was very little I could do to improve the old barnlike house and unsightly grounds, but the more I did the more there was to be done. I began by removing the old overgrown hedge from the side and front of the yard. After grading the ground we sodded the whole yard in Bermuda grass. The house was next underpinned with rough strips of lumber which were painted. A lattice fence was also built from the house to the garage (about 40 feet).

Between the fence and the lawn a space about 30 feet square was left for a flower garden. Just in front of the fence several rambling rose bushes, jonquills, and chrysanthemums were planted. All around the garden I had flower beds about 4 feet wide filled with marigolds, zenias, bachelor buttons, asters, and phlox.

In the summer we decided that we could afford a concrete walk and steps. This was a little expensive but it has helped the looks of the place so much that we have never regretted the time and money spent.

The interior next received attention, beginning with my own room. The furniture consisted of an iron bedstead, an oak dresser, table, and chairs. There was a faded rug on the floor. I moved the dresser to another room, then from an old washstand I made a little dressing table. With rough lumber I made a window seat which I covered with bright cretonne. The furniture was very attractive after a coat of paint and two of enamel were put on. I have very light curtains at the windows. The old rug was turned over and looks almost like new.

The walls in the living room and hall were painted in buff, the dining room and kitchen are to be the same.

One of the greatest improvements of the interior is the built-in cabinets. A very convenient one was made between the dining room and kitchen, where an old chimney used to be. The bricks were used to build a basement. The part of the cabinet in the dining room is to be used for dishes, and that in the kitchen for the cooking utensils. Both are to be painted cream inside and oak outside.

Next spring I am going to plant more flowers and keep working on everything that I think can be improved, for I love home projects. It not only has helped me, but has helped my entire family and even our neighbors.

Section V

ADDITIONAL UNITS IN ART RELATED SPECIFICALLY TO HOUSE FURNISHING AND CLOTHING SELECTION

> Though we travel the whole world over to find the beautiful, we must carry it with us or we find it not.—
> EMERSON.

In the earlier sections of this bulletin it has been suggested that the first course or unit in art be chiefly concerned with the fundamental principles of art and that applications of them be made in a great many fields. It is anticipated that a detailed or complete study of art as related to home furnishing or to clothing selection is to be given at a later time as separate units or courses. It is, however, hoped that the foundation course in art related to the home will give pupils such training that they will be better able to solve their most common daily problems in which art is an important factor, should they fail to have opportunity to take units in home furnishing or clothing selection later.

In schools having two semesters that can be devoted to related art, it is recommended that the fundamental art course in which general applications are to be made be given in the first semester and the work of the second be composed of these more advanced units. When but one semester is provided for related art work, additional units in home furnishing and clothing selection should become a part of the regular homemaking program, with several consecutive weeks planned for each unit. These additional units offer fine opportunity for further applications of the principles of art in judgment and creative problems pertaining to home furnishing and clothing. Since the pupils will have gained an art consciousness through the more general course in art related to the home, and should have developed to a fair degree an ability to recognize and use certain fundamental art principles, it may be expected that the home furnishing and clothing selection units will be built around the larger and more difficult judgment and creative problems of selection, combination, arrangement, and rearrangement as they are met in life.

In planning for a unit in home furnishing as an additional unit in related art, the present and future needs of girls should again be considered. In the study of house plans, the question arises as to whether or not to require pupils either to draw original plans or to copy plans for houses. To do so has been justified as a means of developing interest of pupils in well-planned houses. However, since comparatively few pupils will ever make use of house plans they have made and because many of them will have occasion for making changes in a house that is already planned or assisting in the selection of a plan for a house, it would seem more worth while and less time consuming for them to judge house plans from the standpoint of convenience and the placing of furniture than to draw them. Since the amount and kind of wall space is a determining factor in successful arrangements of home furnishings, opportunity for the individual pupil and class to judge house plans should be provided. Many interesting plans are to be found in nearly all household magazines. Care in the selection of such plans is important in order to avoid discussion of types of houses that are not in keeping with the standards of the community.

If the home furnishing unit is to provide worth-while training and experience it should give to the pupils not only an ability to recognize good design and pleasing proportion in various pieces of furniture but ability to determine pleasing combinations of color, design, and texture in upholstery, drapery materials, and floor coverings, and to arrange and rearrange furniture and home accessories so that the rooms are comfortable and inviting.

In all consideration of home furnishing and accessories, emphasis is given to the selection of the vase, the lamp, the chair, or the curtain which is most pleasing in shape and suited in color and texture for a particular grouping or arrangement. In the earlier and more general art unit, attention is confined to such selection for some parts of the home, but in the later study of home furnishing, they are made for the entire home, with more specific reference to the relationship of one room to another and to larger arrangements.

It is assumed that in classes for the average girl 14 years of age and above, little if any reference will be made to period furniture. If any is made, it should be from the point of view of determining the suitability of adaptations of it to the average home and not purely as a means of identifying one style from another.

To the extent that a better appreciation of good design and proportion in furniture may be gained by studying why some period furniture, as early American, is always beautiful and continues to be reproduced, it may be desirable to make some allusion to it. When a teacher determines that for the majority in a particular class there is no need for devoting any time to a consideration of period styles in furniture, she may satisfy the few who ask questions concerning those styles by directing them to specific reference readings and allowing them to make individual studies of those in which they have greatest interest.

The type of furniture to be found within the community is always a guide in determining how much, if any, study of period furniture is to be made. An attempt to justify such a study is sometimes made from the standpoint of the pupil's personal need in assisting in the selection of new pieces of furniture for the parental home and of the future need in selecting furniture for her own home. But, after all, success in providing an attractive and convenient home depends more upon the harmonious combination of colors and materials and the satisfying daily arrangement of furniture and accessories than upon whether or not the furniture is of a definite period or style. It is upon the former that emphasis should be placed in planning and directing a unit in home furnishing if it is to be of the most service in the everyday experiences of the pupils.

The unit in clothing selection provides further opportunity for valuable art training. The main purpose in this unit is to develop in the pupils an ideal of being becomingly dressed at all times and an ability to choose and combine articles of clothing into attractive daily ensembles. It is evident that if such a training is to be of real service to the pupils in meeting their daily clothing problems they must work as much as possible with actual garments, clothing materials, and clothing accessories. The pupils may be expected to bring some of the needed garments and accessories from home, the teacher may borrow some from the stores, and whenever possible the pupils may be taken to the stores. Such an experience as the last named is most true to life and is described elsewhere under the topic "Field trips." (See pp. 53-55.)

Many teachers question whether or not to include some study of historic costume. Since the unit in clothing selection is designed to give the pupils an ability to solve their daily clothing problems, the practice of having the pupils make sketches, tracings, and mountings of costumes of different periods is undoubtedly of little value. It is not only time consuming but can contribute very little to the development of judgment in selecting and combining articles of modern clothing into suitable and becoming ensembles. There is even a danger that such a procedure may stifle rather than stimulate interest in beautiful and harmonious clothing combinations for everyday use. However, certain features of those costumes which have withstood the test of time and have been revived and adapted again and again in modern dress designs may justly claim some consideration. A few well selected and mounted illustrations of these historic costumes in color may stimulate an interest in art and a desire to know more about the influence of dress in the early periods upon the designs of to-day as well as contribute to better appreciation of color.

Section VI

ILLUSTRATIVE MATERIAL

When you understand all about the sun and all about the atmosphere and all about the rotation of the earth, you may still miss the radiance of the sunset.—WHITEHEAD.

PURPOSE

In home economics teaching there is an increasing recognition of the importance of illustrative material as a teaching device. There is no greater opportunity for effective use of it than in the teaching of art related to the home. Since one of the major objectives of such a course is to develop an ability to select the most suitable materials and articles, and since there is such a variety from which to choose, it is essential that materials which will give the pupils contact with good things and adequate experience in selection be provided. Another important objective is to develop ability to make successful combinations and arrangements. Since it is not yet possible to use real homes as classrooms, it is advantageous to bring some of the home into the schoolroom.

Some outstanding advantages of the use of illustrative material are:

1. It focuses attention upon a single example and affords opportunity for common interpretation and discussion.

2. It furnishes visual as well as audible instruction.

3. It provides contact with actual materials not in an imaginary form, but as found in real life. (The use of doll-size houses with furnishings is questionable for their construction is too time-consuming and they are too much in miniature to furnish standards or to interest girls in real problems.)

SELECTION AND SOURCE

What are the factors governing the choice of illustrative material? The following ones have been adapted from a study by a graduate student at the University of Nebraska. The material should—

1. Make a psychological appeal by—
    a. Coming within the experience of the pupils.
    b. Being suited to their age and previous training.
    c. Possessing pertinent and attractive qualities.
2. Afford wide opportunity for independent choice.
3. Be simple and adapted to the standards of the community.
4. Be reasonable in cost.

Teachers of art have a double problem in the selection of illustrative material in that they must not only choose those things which meet the above standards, but they must eliminate those in which there are unrelated factors which cause a lack of clarity. Quality rather than quantity should be the guide in making selections, for a small amount of well selected and arranged illustrative material is usually more effectively used than a large unorganized collection. Having determined upon the pieces of material that are desirable, the next problem is where to obtain them. Every teacher of art should build up her own personal collection of materials to supplement what can be procured from other sources, for one teaches best from her own material. At the same time, the teacher has a responsibility in guiding the selection of some pieces which should be provided by the school as permanent illustrative material. Still other pieces which it is inadvisable for either teacher or school to buy may be borrowed for special purposes. Chart 3 lists the general types of illustrative material and indicates possible sources of this material.

CHART 3.—*Types and sources of illustrative materials*

General types of illustrative materials	Sources of these materials
I. Articles and materials in everyday use:	

1. School-owned materials—
 	
    Book ends.
    Candlesticks and candles.
    China.
    Colored papers.
    Curtains.
    Flower vases and bowls.
    Necklines cut from neutral fabrics.
    Pictures.
    Screen.
    Swatches of fabrics—
        For color.
        For design.
        For texture.
    Wall hangings.
    Yarns of many colors.
 	
2. Borrowed materials—
 	
    Brass or pewter articles.
	1. This collection will be accumulated as funds are available and as desirable articles are located. Certain things as bits of yarns and scraps of materials may be contributed by members of classes.
	
	2. Borrowed from teachers, homes, and stores in the community.

Wardrobe accessories.
Dresses.
Dressing table articles.
Household linens.
Picture molding samples.
Scarfs.
Small tables.
Table runners.
Trays.

II. Collected and constructed materials:

1. Collected—

Magazine covers.
Magazine advertisements.
Magazine articles and illustrations.
Commercial advertising—
    Booklets.
    Boxes of miscellaneous size and shape.

1. Collected by the teacher from commercial firms and magazines. Much of this material comes to the teacher by virtue of her position and should therefore be considered school property.

Catalogues—
    Wallpaper.
    Furniture.
    China.
    Silver.
    Pictures.
    Floor coverings.
Charts—
    Paints and enamels.
    Fabrics.
    Dyes.
Colored paper samples.
Fabric samples.	

2. Constructed—
 	
Paper models representing—
    Margins.
    Space divisions.
    General proportions.
    Repetition of units.
	2. Made by the teacher.

Harmony of shapes.

Colour wheel.

USE

The above list of illustrative material should in no way be considered as representing all that should be provided for the teaching of art nor as meeting minimum requirements. It is, however, indicative of some of the materials that are desirable and most usable as well as available at a small expenditure of money.

The finest collection of illustrative material is futile if it is not used in such a way that the pupils see the significance of it and develop discriminating powers through the use of it. Charts and other materials lose their value if hung around the room or left in the same arrangements from September to June. Little notice is taken of them for they seem to become a permanent part of the background. Most charts are not decorative and their use should be confined to that part of the work to which they definitely contribute.

There are three important objectives to be kept in mind in the use of illustrative materials. They are—

1. To arouse interest. For this purpose pertinent materials should be arranged attractively on the bulletin board or screen or placed in some conspicuous part of the classroom. These particular pieces should be changed very frequently. See Figure 2, page 8.

2. To assist in solving problems in the development of the principle. The teacher will need to use clear and concise illustrative materials for this purpose. Since these pieces of illustrative material are usually held up before the class, it is necessary that they be of such size that all of the pupils can see them clearly. In addition, the class should be so arranged that all members have equal opportunity for observing them and handling them.

3. To assist in developing judgment ability. Materials for this purpose will be used in two ways: (1) As an aid in solving judgment problems given to the class. In this case some pieces will be used by the group as a whole and others will be passed out to individual pupils. (2) As a means of further developing powers of discrimination and judgment. For this pupils are asked to make selections and arrangements from a large number of articles and materials.

In using illustrative material it is often advisable to have examples of both the good and the poor. When this is true, one must remember to finish with the good. In other words, start with the poor and contrast with the good; or start with the good, contrast with the poor, and then go back to the good.

Illustrative materials can not serve such purposes successfully unless they are so arranged as to be easily accessible for class use. For example, the small fabric sample mounted fast to a sheet of paper can not be examined adequately for texture study. It would be far better to have larger samples which are unmounted, thus making possible not only design, color, and texture study of them, but also many variations in combinations.

The bulletin board and screen, well placed, offer good possibilities for accessibility of certain illustrative material which does not need to be handled. The screen is preferable because it can be moved around and placed to the best advantage for vision and light.

To the extent that pupils have contact and experience with real articles and materials, there will be a better carry over and thus a greater ability to solve everyday art problems successfully.

CARE AND STORAGE

In addition to collecting and using illustrative materials, the teacher has the further problem of caring for and storing them. Soiled, creased, or worn materials are not only lacking in inspiration but set up poor standards.

Illustrative materials may be most efficiently cared for by—

1. Mounting that from which margins will not detract, that in which only one side needs to be used, and that of which texture study is not important.

2. Avoiding too long or unnecessary exposure.

3. Careful handling.

4. Cleaning if possible.

5. Pressing.

6. Labeling and classifying.

7. Careful storing.

Good storage for illustrative materials offers many problems, but is that sufficient excuse for a teacher to leave materials on the wall the year around or piled carelessly on open shelves in the classroom? The provision for adequate storage does not necessarily require elaborate equipment nor a large expenditure of money. Cabinets and steel filing cases are highly desirable but are not absolutely essential for good storage.

Much of the illustrative material for teaching related art lends itself to storage in manila folders and large envelopes, but some could better be stored in boxes, and still others, such as posters, swatches of fabrics held together by large clips, or pictures, may be best hung up.

The use of folders or envelopes necessitates a place to keep them. In the absence of a filing case, one teacher improvised space by utilizing a large, deep drawer. A partition through the center made it possible to arrange two rows of folders. The same plan might be utilized in narrower drawers, providing for one row of folders and space at the side for storage of boxes. If regular manila folders are not large enough to protect the materials, larger ones may be procured at small expense by making them of heavy paper, which is obtainable at any printers. A strip of bookbinding tape may be used to reinforce the bottom.

Cupboard shelves are more often provided in school laboratories than drawers. In such cases large envelopes, which are easily labeled and handled, will hold the materials more successfully. Boxes are very usable also, and may be stacked on shelves for easy accessibility. Those which are uniform in size and color are especially nice for storing many materials such as textiles, yarns, and other bulky pieces, and when used on open shelves a good standard of appearance in the laboratory is maintained.

Any available space for hanging materials can also be used effectively. Textile swatches, charts, and posters, as well as garments, may be kept in better condition by hanging in closets or cases than by packing.

When the teacher of art has the privilege of advising on the original building plans that include an art laboratory, she would do well to plan for various types of storage space. Perhaps the first essential is plenty of drawer space of varying sizes. Shallow drawers of 4 to 6 inches are recommended by many art teachers. These may vary in width and length, but some should be sufficiently large for posters and the larger pictures. Some deeper drawers are desirable for the odd, bulky pieces of material. Cupboards with solid panel doors should also be provided, for boxes, vases, candlesticks, and similar articles which can be most easily stored on shelves. If a storage closet or case is to be provided, a small rod and many hooks should be included. Then, of course, a special series of deep drawers or a filing case for the material that can be placed in folders should be a part of any newly planned laboratory.

The most important factor is accessibility, and therefore the containers for all materials must be plainly labeled and conveniently arranged. Since illustrative material is such a valuable teaching device in art related to the home, good storage space and easy accessibility are of fundamental importance in its successful use.

End